Paul Sams is a practicing property Solicitor actively involved in residential, residential and commercial development with niche specialisms in leasehold enfranchisement matters plus equity release.

Rebecca East is a practicing Solicitor handling all aspects of residential conveyancing particularly new build purchases and equity release.

A Practical Guide to New Build Conveyancing

Second Edition

A Practical Guide to New Build Conveyancing

Second Edition

Paul David Sams

LLB Hons (silver badge in Cycling proficiency)

Solicitor

Specialist in all matters Conveyancing both

Residential and Commercial

Rebecca East

LLB Hons

Law Brief Publishing

Published 2023 by Law Brief Publishing, an imprint of Law Brief Publishing Ltd
30 The Parks
Minehead
Somerset
TA24 8BT

www.lawbriefpublishing.com

Paperback: 978-1-914608-90-2

PREFACE

I would like to dedicate my share in this book to my parents, my partner Ross and to our newborn son Joseph. They all continue to encourage and support me at every opportunity. They collectively make me want to strive to be the best version of myself possible.

I would like to make a special mention to Paul and Sarah Sams. They gave me the chance to join Dutton Gregory when I was not at my most confident. Without their support, time, extensive knowledge and the opportunities Dutton Gregory has afforded me with, I would not be where I am today.

(Rebecca East)

I would like to dedicate this book to the staff and participants at the Rainbow Centre for Conductive Education in Fareham. Since they allowed me to become a trustee nearly seven years ago it has been a privilege to help them all in my own small way. All the proceeds from any of the books I write I have always pledged the same to Rainbow for the amazing work it does. It helps to keep my perspective on life when I see how those without many of the things the vast majority of us take for granted deal with the issues that confront them with a smile on their face.

(Paul Sams)

The law is correct as at 20th February 2023.

Paul Sams & Rebecca East
February 2023

CONTENTS

CHAPTER ONE

INTRODUCTION

Paul Sams & Rebecca East

Congratulations. If you are reading this then you are in the right place. The right place is of course subjective but we like to think that this is a good place to spend some time reading about some riveting stuff about legal issues involving property. We have managed to get our way through a pandemic so a few thousand pages of a section 106 agreement should not phase you should it?

In all seriousness the world has never faced something so uniting in one way but dividing in others as Covid 19. Never before have Governments collectively taken decisions to effectively stop their respective economies which in turn causes financial hardship to their people. In the United Kingdom the respective National and regional Governments/Assemblies have worked together (to some extend) to limit the movement of their citizens to try to stop the spread of what on the face of it is a virus that takes it victims so viciously.

This led to an unprecedented stampede in the housing market in 2020 after June. Many indices suggest that the demand for housing was up fifty-five (55%) compared to 2010. Whether this is true or not I certainly know that unlike my firm and team who are used to being busy, many firms have struggled to cope. The Chancellor's announcement of a temporary stamp duty land tax cut until 31 March 2021 (extended to 30 June 2021 for most and until 30 September 2021 for a few more) led to even more demand. Clients have never had such enthusiasm to complete as we have had in 2020 through to June 2021.

During this time we had people who really wanted to complete transactions. I can understand it. If they wanted to move from one place to another, had found their dream property and had an inkling that they were about to have to stay in one place for some time surely now was the time to do so.

Clients, particularly residential conveyancing clients who are transformed from meek and mild easy going folk into foaming at the mouth rabid animals because they had to leave a message because you dared to cheat on them by speaking to another client when they called, do not care what your internal issues are. They are paying for a service and they expect to get it. Let's face it, we lawyers would be the same if we were in their shoes. However with the deadline of exchange being usually within a set time period for most new build properties this clamour we had during "Covid conveyancing" has always been there with new build property.

The thing is that I predominantly deal with new build property. It is really my thing, in a way I am surprised it has taken me so long to get around to writing a book on the topic. As anyone who knows me will tell you, the thing I am most fond of in this world is the sound of my own voice. It was only really the prompting of the fabulous Miss East (you will hear from her shortly I promise) that I realized it was time I shared my views on new build conveyancing with you all. In fact due to the sales of the first edition this is the new and improved second edition taking into account some of the changes that have occurred since the first edition hit the shelves a couple of years ago.

Well in this book let's take a look at why new build conveyancing is different to dealing with existing properties. I will let you into a major secret now, this does not mean you can stop reading now though, the differences are quite subtle and not really differences at all. Hopefully though that won't put you off reading more.

I will be handling that chapter. I will also be dealing with having a look at new homes warranties, this may come as a shock when you read the same as to the real purpose of the same and also, brace yourselves, there are other providers other than NHBC, they do produce the best flags for site sales though in my opinion. Yours truly will also have a brief look at searches, do you really need them? I appreciate that might make some traditional conveyancers keel over in shock, just like CPSE enquiries are like a childhood Teddy bear hugged for comfort by commercial property lawyers, residential conveyancers do like their searches. If I was an Estate Agent I imagine they would be gazillionaires for the amount of times they have been told that someone was "waiting for searches".

We shall take a look at Help to Buy, described to me in 2019 as the "crack cocaine" of the property market, I will let you have my view on why that view is wrong. Nailing my colours to the mast, I am true capitalist (I know, odd for a fan of the most socialist TV franchise show in history, "Star Trek" to say). I will also provide a brief history lesson in previous incarnations of the same.

Finally but not least, I will take a look at one of the big issues affecting former new build property in Estate charges and the consequences of Section 121 of the Law of Property Act 1925 (800 words in for my Partner Mark Broad). The reference for Mr Broad is how many words could I write before mentioning some law. Being one of my biggest fans when it comes to the books I write (as my wife likes to say possibly the only person who reads them) I think it is only fair I recognize him here.

Well that is enough from me for now. I will now pass you over to the brains behind the operation, Rebecca East. It is a true privilege that she agreed to write this book with me so I will leave you in her capable hands for now to explain what she will be looking at. See you again in Chapter 2.

You would think I would have gotten over my imposter syndrome by now but it is still very much there! After the success of the first edition of this book, it is an absolute pleasure to be back again with an updated version of the same. Once again I would like to extend my gratitude to Paul for affording me the opportunity to co-write this book.

Now I'm not going to sit here and say I have as many years under my belt as the multi-award winning author that is Mr Paul Sams (he will love that I've slipped that one into the book so early on) but what I will say is that I have had my fair share of dealings (including writing the first edition of this book!) to warrant being able to advise on the topic in hand (or at least to explore the dos and don'ts).

Residential Conveyancing is very procedural with the odd bit of law thrown in. Something I wish I would have known when studying Land Law at University. Pretty sure that two-hour lecture on a Friday afternoon scarred me for life but in reality, Conveyancing is actually quite enjoyable (sometimes!) New Build Conveyancing is more procedural I would say. This obviously has its advantages and disadvantages but ultimately it gives you a framework and a timeline to follow, unlike second-hand market properties, so you know where you are and what else you need to do to get from A (pre-exchange formalities) to B (exchange of contracts) and then ultimately completion.

Now unlike Paul, I have never been one to predominantly deal with new build conveyancing. I enjoy the variety that comes with doing a variety of different transactions within the umbrella that is Conveyancing. What I will say though, is that new build conveyancing certainly has a number of advantageous features that I think the second-hand property market could learn from. I am an advocate of streamlining the Conveyancing process wherever possible. It is the fast-paced nature that generally comes with a new build transaction that I love. It is sometimes difficult to explain to a client why there are delays during their transaction. They ultimately want to get to exchange/completion as soon as reasonably possible. Whilst these delays are usually out of the conveyancer's control (search delays, lender's requirements, mortgage offers etc), you are the face of the transaction in hand and therefore, unfortunately, the person to take the brunt of their frustrations! What you have to remember is that you cannot please all of the people all of the time. As long as you're doing your best for your client (and the lender!) that's all that matters. With new build transactions, the timeframe involved to get to exchange tends to be quicker (albeit the property completion might not if it is still in the process of construction!) but at the end of the transaction you are still likely to have a happy client and more importantly happy developer if you hit your exchange deadline!

Our aim in writing this book is to provide a clear practical guide to new build conveyancing and practice. We believe that the future of not just new build conveyancing but conveyancing as a whole lies in greater efficiency from all parties. Dutton Gregory continue to be forward thinking in their approach to not only conveyancing but all areas of law that we practice. We have continued to 5odernize our approach to the way in which we carry out conveyancing transactions making it easier for our clients to track the process of their case. An example of this is the introduction of an app. Our clients will be notified during all key processes to ensure they are fully informed as to what is happening during their transaction. Ultimately communication is key when carrying out all types of conveyancing transactions.

This comprehensive guide seeks to deconstruct the new build conveyancing process, outline the advantages of a new home and explore any potential pitfalls. By the end of this book we hope that the reader will be better served in acquiring a further understanding into the minefield that is new build conveyancing.

CHAPTER TWO

WHAT IS "NEW BUILD CONVEYANCING"

Paul Sams

Many people in life claim to be a specialist. Few ever are. I will make a confession. Really I am a generalist. I do a little bit of everything when it comes to property. In fact, given I spend most of my time leading these days and not dealing with the legal work I am more akin to some lazy bloke in a non-ivory tower. Acting for buyers and sellers of existing properties have been in place for years, listed building, freehold, leasehold, those with mortgages, cash purchases, a bit of commercial property and some residential development acting for the developer then handling sales of the properties that have come from the same. I also handle Equity Release work and some leasehold enfranchisement work.

Writing that down actually makes my head spin a little as I do seem to do quite a lot. Add to that that I am an active Father, husband (Mrs Sams might disagree on the active husband part), Partner in charge of Property for my firm overall, I also lecture other lawyers nationally on various legal issues, write books like this as well as articles and am a Trustee for the Rainbow Centre for Conductive Education in Fareham. My share of the profits from this book will go to Rainbow so please don't feel that by buying this book you are lining my pockets. You are in fact helping an extremely worthwhile cause with people who live with neurological conditions that make simple tasks for most of us harder to deal with.

Now that we have established that I am not a specialist here is where I contradict myself. Yes, a U-turn but given that our Government of the past few years have been accused of the same, in all honesty I would say they have acted quickly to a change of circumstances that was fluid in nature, this though by me is a U-turn. I am a specialist in new build work. For the past 20 years of my working life new build work has dominated my professional career.

To be me it has provided the foundations for the departments I have founded in the three firms I have worked with (and in two cases including my current firm, part owned) be able to grow. Before looking at the practical legal differences in conveyancing when it comes to new property I think it is important to consider the big psychological differences between dealing with a new property compared to an existing property.

Psychological I hear you say? Am I reading the wrong book. No you are not so please bear with me. There is a huge set of psychological differences. Let me explain further.

Many moons ago when I was a young newly qualified solicitor one of the Partners in the firm where I was working asked if I could see a lady who had walked in off the street. Her late husband had been a long standing client of the firm's Corporate team and she had told our receptionist that she wanted to buy a property.

I straightened my tie and went down the two flights of elegant stair cases in the office to meet her. Not sure what to expect I did not expect to see a rather short lady with a battered shopping trolley wearing three quarter length gloves. She explained she was buying a very large property on the Isle of Wight for a not inconsiderable sum. When I asked if she was planning on raising a mortgage to assist with the purchase she said no and handed me over the card of a Director of a well-known prestigious bank.

Not just an area Director mind you but a Director who sat on their international board. I was told to call him and he would provide evidence of her funds if I needed them. It transpired she was enormously wealthy. Purchasing the property was a drop in the ocean for her, mind you where the property she wanted to purchase was right by the sea I could see that literally happening at some point in the future.

The transaction never went through though for two reasons not connected to the property itself. Firstly the sellers were obsessed with trying to find out where my client had her funds from. The sellers had been assured by the Estate Agents who had seen proof of her funds that they need not be concerned. I had also confirmed this to the sellers' solicitors but they kept asking if their client could see it for themselves. In fairness the solicitors themselves seemed embarrassed by their clients' requests.

The second reason that the property feel through was because the sellers demanded that the buyer pay the grand sum of £75.00 for some less than new garden furniture. You know the type, think white plastic that you could pick up just about anywhere. The sort found at Zoos and outdoor venues across the world. The type that would not cost much to purchase brand new.

This request for £75.00 in addition to the considerable purchase price was too much for my client who simply withdrew as she decided she did not like the way the sellers were reacting. She paid my full costs without me having to ask and went on to buy somewhere else.

You may say that was not a particularly interesting story but I use it to highlight the difference between purchasing a new property and an existing one. In the case of most existing properties the person who owns it generally has lived there or has some connection to the property itself, whether that be from renting the same out or selling if for a relative through probate. Either way the seller has an emotional connection to the property and secretly most people want to know that their property, that they may have loved and treasured, will be passed to someone who will treat it as they did.

There is no such emotional connection (or should not be) when the seller of a newly constructed property is selling. This is their business. If they don't sell what they have built then their business fails. That simple, they must sell it. For the large national developers they must sell every single unit they build. Quick sales, fast turnaround, no delays. They produce properties like widgits on a production line so they want them sold. No time for sentiment.

A developer does not have time to decide if they prefer Mr and Mrs X over Mrs and Mr Y as to who will look after the property the most once they have parted with it. They want to know who will pay the most and how quickly they will do it.

It is the speed I think that hovers in most people's minds when dealing with new build property. That applies to both the buyers, sellers and conveyancers. Many conveyancers have said to me over the years they don't like new build because of the time pressures. I love it. Having the mind and attention span of a goldfish then I adore the fast turnaround involved in new build property.

In the immortal words from one of my favourite movies of the 1980's, I feel the need for speed. Given the final release of the sequel to said film last year the phrase always brings a smile to my face.

New build property is all about getting from "a" instruction to "b" exchange as quickly as possible. Nothing else matters. Obviously other things do matter but to all parties this needs to be foremost at the buyer's and the buyer's conveyancers' minds. If you do this then the wheels of industry keep turning.

I have a somewhat horrible phrase that I have said to my teammates within my firm but it is true. That is "seconds or you are dead". In this modern world if you have not dealt with something as soon as it has arrived with you then you a problem.

A developer wants exchange more than anything else. The first word out of a good developer's mouth when they are a babe in arms is not "mama" or "dada" it is "exchange". Followed by the word "now", obscenities may often accompany the same.

There can be no delays. The developer will know, if they are a national developer they probably know more than the security services about your purchaser clients, during the course of their transactions. For example they will call your client to make sure they have returned their instructions to you and paid monies on account. The developer will know that a contract pack has been sent to you because they were either copied in on the email from their solicitors to you or because they have an inhouse legal department like several large national developers have. They will also probably know before you do that your clients mortgage offer has been issued. They will certainly know that the Authority to Proceed under the Help to Buy scheme has been issued to you.

The large amount of information and timing of that information that the developer has about when things happen means you need to be aware of that an act accordingly. Now I can hear some of you saying, "well they are not my clients" and that is very true. However they have influence over your client so if you want an easier life it can be best to keep that in mind. I am some of you are horrified by these comments and are of the view that your role is to protect your client. That is fine for you to have that view. It is true. However I am a realist and a capitalist at heart. Completing transactions generates funds for your firm which in turn pay your salary or drawings. The huge number of lawyers who whilst intelligent people cannot grasp that firms survive based on the fees they generate genuinely horrifies me.

So if you want to be considered good at new build conveyancing you need to be considered quick. Quick and good can happen. Some will tell you they are mutually exclusive comments but they are wrong. The same can be good bed fellows. That is because during their "courtship" quick and good need to be introduced to each other by another word. Organised. As with anything else, being organised goes a long way to getting things done. I am blessed that I have had some great lawyers and assistants work with me over the years. Putting aside Miss East's huge ability then I have to give a special mention to Amy Briscoe who is by far one of the best I have had the privilege to work with. Super organized and rarely stressed she never ceases to amaze me.

So as I have alluded to organisation is the key. "How do I get organised?" I hear you ask. Like the boy scouts, be prepared. If you are going to be dealing with a lot of purchasers on a single site, let me share a secret with you. The title to each property will be roughly the same. There will be subtle differences but you can probably use the same report for all with a few tweaks as and when needed. You could even, I appreciate this may shock some conveyancers so take a deep breath, use the same report on the same site for freehold and leasehold properties. Changing the section on whether it is a flat or a house to include the major details we all tend to report on (each schedule in a transfer/lease with a summary is how I do things). Something I should have pointed out in edition one which I will now, make sure you are aware of changes to the site papers as it is key that you do actually update any master reports that you hold.

Well with that bombshell let me share another secret. Try to get on with the conveyancer acting for the developer. This is not combat blood sports and there is no point trying to score points from the lawyer on the other side.

Now I know sometimes I have had some run-ins with people on the other side. I admit in the past twelve months snapping at some quite frankly awful Licenced Conveyancer via email who insisted on copying her client into every email she sent me with enquiries (including wanting a peppercorn ground rent provision being amended as it did not state it would not increase in the future – that was not the worst one she sent me either). However once we exchanged she insisted on telling me that clearly I had not been loved as a child. She made a point of telling me this after exchange. I was tempted to send her a copy of one of my books but since there are no pictures in them she may struggle. The Estate Agent has indicated that their client will never be using that Conveyancer again as they were awful to deal with so that is something I suppose. By the way this is not a slight against Licenced Conveyancers either. They could easily have been a solicitor, legal executive, barrister or Barista.

However if you get on with the person on the other side of you it will make things much easier for you and your client. I have been lucky to deal with some great conveyancers for developers over the years. Janice Taylor, Louise Patterson, Zoe Owen, Rebecca Price and Gareth Fullbrook to name but a few. In fact Gareth now works with me so I no longer get to exchange with him on a Saturday morning. Although I did exchange contracts with Zoe once when I was in the queue at the Fish n Chip shop on a Friday evening. Getting on with your opposite number will help in many ways.

For starters they will probably highlight any changes to their client's paperwork to you so you don't have the surprise of spotting it when you do your next report. You can use them as a conduit to keep their client informed of issues that might be arising with your client. For example if your client is having issues with an associated sale then your client (and the developer) would benefit from amending an unrealistic demand to exchange on a certain date. Moving that date should not prove too much of an issue as at the end of the day developers, as I have alluded to earlier, do not have the emotional attachment that other sellers may have.

Of course sometimes you will have a problem no one has foreseen. The obligatory IT failure, power cut, flood and banking system crash, having been through all of these scenarios my "crisis bingo card" is fully ticked off. Having someone be your advocate does you no harm. We all need friends in the law so can I suggest that your opposite number be that for you.

I have alluded to above the time frames. The biggest difference some might say between resale conveyancing and new build property is the stipulation of an exchange time frame. There may be time frames imposed on resale properties but I can honestly say that these do as a rule seem to be ignored. One well respected Estate Agent I know always says "the matter will happen when it happens". Those words are horrific to a developer. I know he has said it to many a developer over the years.

Most developers issue a four week-exchange deadline. Some say 21 days, some say 28 days and some say 35 days. Whatever the deadline is the developer will issue one. More importantly they will expect that deadline to be met. If not your client runs the risk of losing the property. Remember when the property market is buoyant a developer is likely to be far more bullish when it comes to deadlines and sticking to them.

I dealt with a developer many years ago that has to this day one of the best sales progressors in this country. Her ruthlessness though knows no bounds. She expects matters to exchange on time and if they don't woe betide you and your clients. Exchange is what she is paid to ensure happens and she will do anything, and I mean anything, to make sure that happens.

Please keep in mind that for a corporate developer they are not like an estate agent. They are not making money from conveyancing referral fees, financial services commissions, commissions from carrying out removals or letting property. A developer's sole income comes from buying land then developing property on that land. It must be built then sold before they can move on to the next one. The daily number of exchanges must be reported from the regional office to the group office to the national board who then need to sweet talk not just their bank but the stock market. That one property you are dealing with can have an influence on their share price which in turn affects the national share index. No pressure but your holding up that exchange could make a difference to the national economy so do think on.

To help with speed can I encourage all of you to have a seamless onboarding process for clients. Now personally I hate the term onboarding but instruction process does not really cut it these days. I hate it when potential clients call and say that "the site sales team have told me to instruct you so am calling you to do that". Now I know this is done with the best of intentions but returning the forms, hopefully via electronic means, paying monies on account and providing identification documents are not yet really possible from a simple telephone call. Getting your client instructed early, it is now something that can be done on day one of opening a file for them, is really key to having everything in place to meet any deadline.

Now everyone has a different way of doing this but I am a fan of electronic identification checks because it is harder to fool a computer system than it is a human being when it comes to false identification. Can you honestly tell me if you would spot a fake passport as I am not sure I could? Electronic identification checks and the use of secure portals to check that your client is who they say they are (and are not a dreaded "P.E.P") helps with conveyancing in general not least the speed element.

Personally I have always advocated reporting to a client with contract papers on a new build property as quickly as you can after receipt of contract papers from the developers solicitors. The client feels involved in the process that something is happening and you have done all you can on the file at that stage.

At a previous firm it was a requirement that all new starters and those who had failed to achieve their time posting target the year before attend a seminar presented by the then senior partner. He was hugely respected chap who had been considered one of the best "billers" that firm had ever had. His mantra was quite simple and I am huge believer in it. When you work on any file does as much on it as you can before you place it back. Don't do half of what you can do. Do it all and then you are less likely to miss something later on. Simple task but I whole heartedly believe in the same. If you follow this you are less likely to go wrong.

Now in the report I am not going to tell you what to include but would make the following suggestions. For starters if you have engrossments get them signed now. Make sure you cover the legal title to the property, any estate charge or service charge that needs to be paid, what new homes warranty that the property may have, searches (or lack thereof), planning documents and finances.

Now you won't be able to exchange until you have mortgage instructions (assuming you are getting a mortgage and your client wants to wait for their mortgage offer before committing to exchange), the authority to exchange under the Help to Buy scheme (see the later chapter on the same) and any associated sale or part exchange. However if you report early so you have a signed contract and have warned the client you will need their deposit to exchange (it never ceases to amaze me the number of clients who are shocked by the request for monies to exchange), this should make life easier to get to exchange.

Another thing I always include in my report with the contract is the engrossment fee that the developers' solicitors will inevitably charge for providing the final documents at completion. Now this can vary between £50.00 to £400.00 plus VAT. Now this has been commonplace for as long as I can remember (I am getting on in years) and in the past few years developers certainly make sure that buyers are told about this at reservation. However still to this day I get asked, usually at completion to be honest "what is this engrossment fee?".

The engrossment fee is to put it bluntly, your client paying the developers solicitors for preparing then final signed transfer or lease. To be even more blunt, paying part of the seller's solicitors' legal fees. I cannot dress this up in any other way. It is part of the convention that is in place for developers and I don't see it changing any time soon.

Some developer's solicitors take it to a new extreme and charge for acknowledging notice of transfer and mortgage at completion. I do find this one a touch unfair for the buyer as the developer's solicitors know who the buyer is as they have provided a lease/transfer with their name in it plus their client has all their contact details! However this is not the format to begin a debate about whether that should change.

The issue I find with the engrossment fee is that no matter that the developer will have told the buyer about the same and you will have told the buyer about the same it more often than not does not get through to the buyer. When they see the completion statement at completion they always seem to query the Estate charge (see a later chapter dedicated to the same) and engrossment fee. "What is this?", "no one told me about this" and "really? Are you sure" are some of the frequent comments I have seen.

Believe me I have tried many different ways over the years of explaining the same. Bold font in the report, coloured text, repeating it more than once in the report letter. Nope, people still keep missing the same. If anyone has any great ideas I have not tried then please feel free to share the same.

Having mentioned earlier in this chapter the need for exchange above all else from a developer's perspective this brings is on to the most different, in my opinion, aspect of dealing with a new build property compared to that of a resale – the completion date.

Those who have ready my book on "Covid Conveyancing" (thank you by the way for your support) will know how scathing I have been over so called "covid clauses". Said clauses seek to destroy the one thing that an exchange of contracts is supposed to bring, certainty to all parties. The idea of exchanging is to let all parties know that they are committed to the transaction, they can then make plans accordingly and a date when completion will take place is agreed for a date in the future both parties agree.

That does not tend to happen with new build properties. Unless the property is build complete then a fixed date will not be agreed for completion. Now under the Consumer Code for House Builders (again more of this in a later chapter) certain time frames have to be agreed but they are fairly wide. More importantly there is no agreement between the parties. The developer makes it clear what they are offering and that is it, take it or leave it.

Now over the years I have realized that some developers sales staff are more keen to point out time frames to buyers than others. That is simply human nature. However that does not stop me feeling like the Grinch when I have to point out that it is likely to be much longer than they had been lead to believe. Now do not get me wrong I am not blaming the site sales staff here. Quite often they have been led to believe by construction staff that a certain date is possible.

In turn the construction personnel will have been told the same by the Construction Director in conjunction with the technical department who will in turn have been told this by suppliers or utility providers. The issue with building a new property is that so many people and factors come into play that one small delay can have a knock-on effect to the whole process. For instance the delays with construction workers being off sites during the height of Covid at the end of March/beginning of April in 2020 delayed some build schedules by months. "Ripples in a pond" is a phrase I am fond of saying as you do not know what those ripples may touch or effect. The fact that we have had the energy crisis since then coupled with war in Europe then the "supply chain" issues we have all been encountering are just getting worse.

Now when it comes to exchange on a new build it is likely that the buyer will be presented with an anticipated legal completion date. That will be a date in the future. Inevitably it will probably be at the end of a month or the last Friday of a month albeit that is not actually a requirement just what tends to happen in practice.

There will either be a long-stop date or a termination period offered. Taking a long stop date that is as it sounds. Completion has to be by a certain date or the contract is rescinded, the buyer can ask for their deposit back and compensation.

Termination period are similar but rather than a specific date being given a range of dates (either two, four or six month) are given to the buyer. How I personally tend to deal with this is by adding the following paragraph to my report letter that accompanies the contract:

"The final moving or completion date is defined within the contract as taking place within 10 days of a notice served by the developers' solicitors upon us to confirm that the property is ready for final valuation and is structurally complete. It is for this reason that we stress you monitor the build programme closely and avoid booking holidays when the developer will expect you to complete. In addition if your lender requires a re-inspection then the more notice that the valuer can have then the less chance of a complication with the valuation.

The developer has not provided an anticipated completion date at the time of compiling this report.

The contract is subject to what is known as a termination period. In this case the termination period is for six months. This means that if at exchange of contracts the anticipated completion for say 30 June 2023 then they could move completion forward by up to six months (1 January 2023) or back by six months (30 December 2023). If completion has not taken place by the end of the termination period then the seller would be in breach of contract to you and you could in turn look to take action against them for any losses you have suffered. Ultimately you could look to regain your deposit and cease to buy the property."

I am not saying that this is always the best way to get the message across to buyers but I do find that it works the majority of the time. It is worth pointing out that in my experience it is rare for developers to go past the long stop or termination period. As stated earlier, developers have to build and then sell what they produce, if they do not, they do not make any money. No money no business. On that basis most large developers make sure they build on time to avoid such issues.

Now I am not saying that happens all the time as I have seen on occasion sites that have gone over the termination period or long stop. It has generally been down to mismanagement from the developer or some catastrophic issue caused elsewhere on a site. However again on a handful of occasions I have seen a developer deliberately go over the termination period or long stop.

Why I hear you ask? Did you not say they have to build and sell to survive. Well yes I did. However as a commercial entity if they have constructed a property that they could sell for a lot more, then the temptation to allow one buyer to withdraw, paying them compensation so they can sell for a lot more, then I can see the commercial decision behind it. I would like to point out this is very rare as for starters a developer does not want to get a reputation for doing this with the public who could be future buyers. Nor do they wish to highlight issues to mortgage lenders who could consider against lending against their properties in the future. The same applies to Homes England who administer Help to Buy. A developer would hate to have to go "cold turkey" from losing their Help to Buy funding line.

So I have looked at time frames and the absolute requirement of a swift exchange but I have not looked at one of the big differences with new build conveyancing which I think we will see more of for the next few years. Part exchange. Developers will often take a buyer's existing property in part exchange to allow them to sell one of their new shiny properties to the buyer. Car dealers do this on new cars and it works well so why not developers. There are many companies across the UK set up to assist developers with part exchange properties. In fact some will actually buy the property for the developer so they do not have to own the same.

Please keep in mind that a developer has a major advantage over most home buyers. Under the Finance Act governing Stamp Duty Land Tax (SDLT) then a developer does not have to pay SDLT when taking a property in part exchange. Provided the seller has used the property as their main residence then the developer will not have to pay SDLT. This can be a large saving depending on the value of the property. Now I am not saying that a developer will not take a former buy to let property for instance in part exchange but their offer for that property will factor in the fact that they have to pay SDLT.

Now I always used to be under the belief that a developer would only take a property in part exchange if the part exchange property was worth only seventy percent (70%) of the new property so that there is a thirty percent (30%) difference between the two. For example if the new property is being sold for one hundred thousand pounds (£100,000.00) then the part exchange property cannot be worth more than seventy thousand pounds (£70,000.00).

However that belief has been tested over the years. I always recall that a friend of mine who was Sales Director for a national developer called me at a weekend to ask if I could quote buyers he had for a million pound (£1,000,000.00) sale he had agreed on one of his swanky new penthouse apartments. He explained it was a part exchange. After the third time of asking he managed to get my disbelieving ears to hear that he was offering than one million and fifty thousand for their current property (£1,050,000.00).

I always remember saying "but that does not work, you are paying them". He replies calmly "Don't worry Paul, it works on paper" to which I replied "what sort of paper, Martian??". That sale and purchase did go through. In two weeks from start to finish if I recall correctly. The developer "had money" in the plot which allowed them to offer such a keen deal. They sold the part exchange property for seventy-five thousand pounds (£75,000.00) more which allowed them sufficient funds to cover their costs involved with the transaction. On reflection now I have to applaud the sales director for doing something so audacious.

The sales pitch that a developer makes to any prospective buyer with a part exchange is elegantly simple. They point out they are a cash buyer, magic words that Estate Agents and society as a whole hammer into people. I would temper that though that few people have a six-figure sum lying around in their current account so remember that famous phrase about all that glitters is not gold.

A developer will also mention that great panacea that society and Estate Agents love to play upon, there will be no chain. Now chains of transactions are somewhat unique in England and Wales compared to elsewhere in the world. I am not saying that this is bad nor am I saying here that other systems are better. I merely wish to place on record that we have a system and it works. It might not work as well as we want it to but it does work. Therefore we just have to accept it.

Now the developer has established they are not getting a mortgage (buyer hears delay when they hear mortgage, waiting for the buyer to get approval then waiting for a survey etc (but see below)) and that there is no chain they are beside themselves with joy. A buyer who will take the property as is, no haggling over the curtains and no waiting for funds to be in place, they are happier than a pig in you know what.

Then along comes the likes of me who have to give them the solemn news. They have the most fastidious buyer that they could ever face. One who will leave no stone unturned in the questions they will ask. Far from having an "easy ride" they will be tortured over every element of their property.

I make no excuse for saying this. I say it because this is the reality that someone undertaking a part exchange transaction has to prepare themselves for. Every developer I know who deals with part exchange wants a gas safety certificate. Not a service certificate or evidence of installation of the boiler (although they will want that to) but a certificate akin to a landlord's safety certificate that would be obtained if a property was rented out to a tenant.

The logic behind this is that the developer does not want to have to replace a faulty boiler. They want the property to be perfect so checking the boiler and having a certificate to say it is safe is an absolute must. In addition there is a trend now for many developers dealing with a part exchange to asking for a full electrical test of the property. Neither a landlord's gas safety inspection or electrical test are requirements under the conveyancing protocol for the sellers to provide but developers want them.

Every developer that makes such demands makes it clear in their reservation process and most follow up with a separate letter to say to buyers they should have this done. Sadly in my experience most buyers seem to fail to get this message. Whether that is because it is not made clear enough or simply it is lost amongst the thousand other things rushing through someone's head when purchasing a new property, well I do not know but it often fails to get through. It is left to us as the conveyancers to make this clear to them what they need to do.

Some developers require that all ground rent and service charge on a leasehold property is paid for twelve months in advance before they will consider exchange. Now whilst they will of course repay the monies due to the buyer at completion by way of apportionment it is quite a lot to pay up front.

My top tip when dealing with a part exchange transaction or in fact a resale transaction where the buyer is also selling is simply to tell your client this. Forget about the new shiny property you want to purchase. Focus on your sale. If you don't concentrate on the sale they will not get the new property. A very simple message but I think it is worth spelling out.

One other major difference comes from the magic form that can be so difficult to get hold off which is all important in new property. What is this mystical form you ask? Well that would be the disclosure of incentives form.

Rather like selling a new car developers like to offer incentives to buyers. Unlike cars you might not get a satellite navigation upgrade but you might receive from the selling developer some form of incentive to make the property more attractive to you. That could include covering your Estate Agents costs for an associated sale, a contribution towards legal costs, a contribution towards stamp duty land tax costs, a "cash" incentive (it is never a wheelbarrow full of funds) to many other options.

Those new to new build conveyancing are often perplexed by this. Having had it drummed into them that any variation or offer of incentive to a buyer is pretty much forbidden without the consent of the mortgage lender this seems to be permitted and dare I say it often encouraged by lenders on new properties. A lot of mortgage lenders will actively state in their mortgage offer that they are aware of incentives and they are fine by them.

The reason they aware is that usually their valuer has seen the form. The form itself is readily available via the UK Finance Mortgage Lenders

Handbook for Conveyancers online. The form was previously known as the Council of Mortgage Lenders disclosure of incentives form or as I save it in my case management system CML DOI form. The current form has been in existence since August 2018.

The original CML DOI form was created in September 2008. Having discussed the same with all the participants in the new homes process which included developers themselves, surveyors, lender and warranty providers the form was decided upon to improve the flow of communication between all parties thus speed up the process. I believe the correct word is transparency. The idea about the form is that incentives are fully disclosed as there was a suggestion in the past that they were not.

The seller should complete this and make sure that the lenders solicitor which inevitably most of the time is the solicitor acting for the borrower has sight of the form showing the incentives. The valuer only has to see this if they request it however most do as they are instructed by the lender to see it to assist them with understanding the value of the property.

The form should be disclosed to the lender by their solicitor unless of course the lenders says they don't need to see it if they already know the incentives. If of course the incentives change then the lender needs to be sent a copy of the revised form to confirm they are happy with the same. A generic rule that all lenders seem to have adopted (although not all) is that incentives should not be more than five (5%) percent of the purchase price.

Now the form is pretty straightforward but they are eleven (11) pages of guidance notes so that should give you an idea of the detail involved. Buyers do not need to see the form itself but it is important that the buyer's solicitors have this. Now I have dealt with developers who have said, "don't worry you don't need a copy of the form there are no incentives" well you still need the form. Even if there are no incentives you need to see this form. So make sure you have it.

Now I admit I am at a loss as to why a mortgage lender will accept up to 5% of the purchase price being offered as an incentive on a new build property. In essence this means that the buyer is only paying ninety-five (95%) percent of the actual purchase price which in turn means that the lender is technically taking a higher loan to value against the property. However convention it seems allows this so you need to be aware that it exists and is likely to be acceptable to the lender.

This does mean though that you need to check the lenders instructions carefully to make sure you comply with the same. Some lenders state in their instructions that they don't want to hear about incentives provided they are not more than five (5%) percent of the purchase price. However a lot of lenders will accept no incentives so please do not make an assumption and check. This nuance over incentives is possibly the biggest difference in new build conveyancing compared to dealing with existing properties.

So we have looked at the major differences between dealing with a new property and a resale transaction in this chapter. In the next chapter we will consider planning permissions and building regulations approval and how to ensure the necessary compliance is in place.

CHAPTER THREE

PLANNING AND BUILDING REGULATIONS

Rebecca East

One of my favourite things about new build conveyancing remains to be that you're given a pack of information from the developer's solicitor from the outset containing the necessary planning and building regulations paperwork (amongst other things!) to enable you to report to your client early on. You tend to find that you will be given the link or access code to the documents by email before you've even had chance to open your own file! Efficiency in conveyancing is so important.

If I had a pound for every time I asked a client on a second-hand property sale if they held *any* of the paperwork from when they purchased (only a handful of years earlier) for them to answer with a confused "no" I'd be a very rich lady! I definitely think the property market generally should have a portal where all relevant paperwork is uploaded to on each property purchase to assist conveyancing practitioners. This is a whole different bug bear of mine! That being said, this share file or hub of information aims to serve as a massive advantage for new build transactions and what ultimately contributes to conveyancing practitioners being able to work towards such tight exchange deadlines.

So you've opened your file, client has returned their instruction forms and now you need to work your way through the 60-odd documents you've been sent by the developer's solicitor. Where do you even start? Personally, I start by reading through the information sheet given by the developers solicitor to familiarise myself with the development. I take particular interest in the planning permission, building regulations and new homes warranty section of the information sheet (aside from obviously doing a title check which is of equal to or more importance!) The starting point when looking at the planning permission for the construction of the property is first to ensure it has been obtained (may seem stupid for me to even suggest this but you can never assume!) and secondly to ensure the property has been constructed in accordance with the submitted plans. When a property is part of a new estate (as with the majority of new homes) the planning permission will refer to the estate as a whole and not individual plots. Not all properties on the development will be built exactly the same albeit that they fall under the same planning permission so you will need to ensure that the relevant property has been built in accordance with the permission (i.e that of a semi-detached property compared to that of a coachhouse).

You are unlikely to have discharge/approval to all planning conditions at this stage especially if the property forms part of a large ongoing development. What you will need to check is what conditions have been met or discharged and which ones are outstanding, what timeframe for being able to comply with these and whether you need to draw your client's attention to them.

When the Local Authority is considering passing Planning Permission, they are likely to consider the requirements or obligations a developer must adhere to in order that the relevant Permission is passed for the development. This is especially important if the development will have a significant impact on the local area that cannot be moderated by simply imposing planning conditions attached to the Planning Permission. The Local Authority will consider the impact the development might have on the social and economic infrastructure which already exists in that area. The obligations imposed in a Section 106 Agreement will seek to balance the pressure created by the new development by ensuring it makes a positive contribution to the local area and the community.

As you're likely to already be familiar with, planning obligations under Section 106 of the Town and Country Planning Act 1990 are a mechanism used by the Local Authority which make a development proposal acceptable in planning terms. Hence my earlier comment about planning being subjective.

Common planning obligations include; to secure affordable housing, specifications on the type and timing of this housing and to secure financial contributions for infrastructure or affordable housing. These are just a few examples of the use of a Section 106 agreement. Other examples can include;

1. Placing restrictions on the development in terms of use of land
2. The requirement for specified operations to be carried out in, on or under the land or
3. The requirement for financial contribution to be paid to the Local Authority or on a specified date or dates.

It is important to note that is the above agreement is not complied with, it is enforceable against the person that entered into the obligation and any subsequent owner. Yes, that would include your client! Some agreements specify that obligations and financial contributions do not fall to the individual property owner but not always. It is therefore the responsibility of the conveyancing practitioner to ensure that this has either been paid and obligations adhered to, is in the process of being paid or complied with or does not fall on the individual property owner. I find this point especially difficult to explain to my client the importance of during a second-hand property purchase. This point almost always carries delays on resales when the specific Section 106 Agreement is not immediately available for review OR it does not specify that it is not binding on an individual property owner and you have to get a third party involved (usually the local authority!) to seek clarity on. As a result it might be worth drawing your client's specific attention to it during their new build purchase so they're not faced with delays during their eventual sale of the same property.

I consider the decision of whether the Local Authority agrees to grant Planning Permission to be subjective whereas the decision of Building Regulations is objective. The required works either comply and therefore the necessary certification is passed for the purposes of Building Regulations or if it fails to meet the required standards it will fail. A very black and white decision.

The Regulations are very detailed and are in place to ensure adequate standards of building work, and to impose the minimum standards required including that for energy conversion and health. Once the works have been completed in accordance with the plans originally submitted by the Local Authority, the developer will seek from the Local Authority (or other professional body facilitating building control sign off) a final certificate. As with Planning permission, this may cover a number of properties. Once the property has been signed off and is fit for occupation you should supply your client with a copy of the final certificate and advise them to keep safe for their eventual sale (together with the other purchase paperwork of which they will likely ignore, forget or lose soon after they move in!) as this certificate confirms that the property has met the required level of satisfaction of the Local Authority (or provider) and in accordance with the Regulations. You will most likely have seen the Daily Mail report stories such as "my property is worthless" or the likes due to lack of the necessary certification. The onus is on you as conveyancing practitioner acting for the purchaser to check this is provided on or before completion. Sounds daft to even suggest this but you'd be surprised!

Moving forward we will now look at the Community Infrastructure Levy Charge or CIL as it is more commonly known. This is a planning charge introduced by the Planning Act as a tool for Local Authorities to use in support for development in that area.

Any development site which creates a new additional floor space of 100 square metres or more, or creates a new dwelling would be potentially liable for the levy charge. CIL only applies in certain areas where a Local Authority has consulted on, and approved a charging schedule which sets out the rates applicate. The schedules can be found on the Local Authority's planning website for avoidance of doubt.

Whilst some developments may be eligible for exemption from the levy, larger new build development sites would have a CIL charge in place. You will want to ensure that this has been paid before completion. Confirmation tends to be given in the pack of information given from the outset but if you cannot locate the same it is always worth raising this as an enquiry for confirmation. Landowners are ultimately liable for the payment of the CIL, but anyone involved in a development may take on the liability to pay. As Paul has said above, if you're lucky enough to build up a good working relationship with the conveyancing practitioner acting for the developer you can raise enquiries on anything you're not sure about without feeling like an absolutely idiot. It is always better to ask the question (and look a bit daft now!) than to risk missing such a vital point which would cause other repercussions if things go wrong later down the line. As with all conveyancing transactions, the onus is on you as buyer (and buyer's lawyer) to make sure the necessary searches, surveys and or personal inspections are done and results satisfactory.

Once I've checked the Planning Permission, Building Regulations and CIL liability I next move onto the position with the roads and footpaths fronting the property or required for access to and from the property. I again start by reviewing the position given in the information sheet provided by the developer together with that mentioned in the Transfer Deed (and accompanying plan) for confirmation.

As you will already be aware, an adopted road is one that is maintainable at public expense. What you will find with the majority of new build developments (including those build within the last 5 years) is that the road is unlikely to be adopted by the Local Authority and will therefore initially be the responsibility of the developer. Not all roads will be adopted and maintained at public expense by the Local Authority however. It is now more common to see private roads fronting new build properties of which the responsibility for day-to-day maintenance and repair will fall to management companies and/or managing agents.

Private, as it sounds, means that they are maintained privately from the Local Authority either by residents or by a management company set up for the purpose of maintenance and repair of the road. They may also maintain other common areas on the new development such as lighting or recreational areas. Contributions towards the cost of maintenance and repair will be by way of Service Charge. Anyway I digress – essentially as long as there is a legal right of way over a road serving to access the property and there are adequate provisions for maintenance this is perfectly acceptable. For the purpose of this chapter I will mainly be focusing on the procedure involved when looking at that of a new road becoming an adopted highway by the Local Authority.

Road adoption is the process involved where a road in private ownership (developer's ownership) becomes a public road, which is then managed and maintained by the Local Authority, as part of the public highway provided if it is constructed to adoptable standards in terms of layout and construction. The process of roads becoming public highways is covered under a road bond. A road bond is a financial guarantee between the Local Authority/Highways agency and the developer which will state that unless the road is complete and constructed to the required standard the Local Authority/Highways authority can use the money to finish it.

There are two main ways in which a new road may be offered for adoption to become maintainable at the public expense.

1. The developer may complete the construction of the road and then offer it to the Highway Authority under Section 37 of the Highways Act 1980; or (and more commonly)

2. The developer enters into a legal agreement under Section 38 of the Highways Act 1980.

I can hear you say *"that's all good and well saying that Rebecca but what exactly is the difference"*. Now I will try to keep this as succinct and brief as possible but essentially a new road will be considered by the Local

Authority for adoption under a Section 38 Agreement of the Highways Act 1980 provided the following criteria are met;

- *it must be of sufficient utility to the public and offer wider community benefits*
- *the roads offered for adoption will have other uses other than simply providing access to residential or commercial properties.*
- *the road will remain open to the public to pass and re-pass at all times when formally adopted*
- *the carriageway and footways offer safe passage for pedestrians and vehicles*
- *the carriageway and footways have an approved mechanism for surface water drainage*
- *street lighting must comply with current local requirements and national standards*
- *they are constructed to a satisfactory standard*

Adoption of the road under a Section 37 agreement allows the developer to construct the road and complete the development without the need for a formal road agreement. Now provided the road is of sufficient standard and is of use to the public other than just to serve access to and from the property (to justify the cost of it being maintained at public expense), the Highway Authority would accept the notice of proposed dedication by the developer and following a 12-month maintenance period the road would automatically become maintainable at the public expense. As mentioned above however, this is not used as often compared to that of the Section 38 agreement.

So I've dealt with Section 37 and 38 agreement but what is a Section 278 agreement? A Section 278 agreement is a section of the Highways Act

1980 that allows developers to enter into a legal agreement with the Highways Authority to make permanent alterations or improvements to a public highway, as part of a planning approval. Section 278 works to the existing highway can be onerous in terms of cost and requirement for the necessary consents. This agreement is generally required where planning permission has been granted for a development that requires improvements or changes to, public highways. As a result these tend to feature early in the developers planning decisions.

The reason why a Section 278 agreement would feature early in the developer's decision making is because the developer may be responsible for carrying out and paying for the works to the satisfaction of the Highways Authority. They may also be liable for any additional costs if they need to modify the highway to suit the development they are building.

In addition to the cost, the developer may have to enter into a bond (agreement) to cover the local Highway Authority against the possibility if the developer is unable to complete the roads to the required satisfaction. This may be due to the developer going insolvent or other situation where the developer could not fulfill the obligations. The bond will be released in stages until a twelve-month maintenance period has elapsed after the works are finalised. If the developer fails to make the required payments or cannot fulfill the obligations it agreed to, the highways authority has the power to close access to the site.

Section 278 Agreements are often entered into alongside Section 38 Agreements. This enables developers to ask the Highway Authority to adopt the new roads along with associated infrastructure such as new drains, lighting and other supporting structures.

If you've dealt with the sale of a second-hand market property that has been built within the last 5 years you will likely know the pain of the dreaded enquiry from a buyer's solicitor regarding the unadopted road fronting the property. Whilst a Section 38 agreement will require the developer to complete certain works within prescribed timescale, sometimes there are delays in completing this. With some larger new build developments, they often encompass a large network of footpaths and roads and can often comprise more than one developer. For ease, the Local Authority divide these into phases. This poses a problem as the phases will be completed in different stages and this can result (as it has in my local area) that the roads are built to the required standard but cannot be adopted by the Local Authority until the other connecting road are also completed to an adoptable standard. In the situation where there is an absence of suitable agreement, the conveyancing lawyer should look to the Transfer Deed from the original developer to the first property owner as there should be a suitable indemnity covenant (albeit it likely being a positive covenant) for road adoption which (in an ideal scenario) should cover successors in title and their lenders.

Following on from that of Planning and Building Regulations approval, it seems only right to explore new homes warranties next. I will therefore hand over to Paul for the next chapter. Over to you Paul.

CHAPTER FOUR

NEW HOMES WARRANTIES

Paul Sams

Developers use these as part of their sales technique. A resale property does not have a new homes structural guarantee but "our property does". As a society we adore feeling safe and any form of insurance we seem to lap up. Recently I purchased a new car and the garage as part of their due diligence (mountains of paperwork for them, poor souls) including offering me key insurance in case I lost of my keys to the car and had to replace them. On the basis that if I lost one key I would use the replacement safely stashed away from the car or my phone which has an app to start the car I politely declined the offer of the same. However when asking they told me that a lot of people do take them up on the same for a variety of reasons. I have to say they nearly persuaded me to until my reality check system told me it was not worth it. Wished the same one kicked in when I am at charity auctions, that Dads Army montage I bought several years ago is bound to be worth more one day surely?

However new homes structural warranties are something that differentiate new build property from those already in existence. The thing is though do you know why they really exist, the history behind the same, what they actually cover and the subtle differences between the various providers now plus why the UK Finance Council of Mortgage Lenders Handbook require the same? Well sit back and relax. I will take you on a journey in relation to the same now. Think of it like that well-loved historical piece about the Royal family on one of the many online streaming platforms, just without royalty and less scandal. I say less scandal but there has been a fair amount involved with new homes warranties in a way.

Let me transport you back to the 1930's. This was a time after the "Great War" that had ended in 1918 and before the outbreak of hostilities that we now refer to collectively as World War two. Some consider it a golden age.

In the 1930's there was major Government concern about poor house building standards that were the result of slum clearance programmes and the inter-war housing explosion of new properties being constructed. However, limited availability of human beings to carry out the work and skills needed in various trades, financial pressures and general incompetence lead to poor building practices. Remember the nursery rhyme about the three little pigs, well think of construction worse than any of the three could come up with. As there was a hurry to build and pressures to make it succeed then corners were cut leading to many issues including sadly some deaths when newly built properties of the time collapsed with their occupants within them. The outcry was loud in the national press so action was needed.

In order to avoid legislation in 1936 the building industry created an organisation called the National House Builders Registration Council (NHBRC). In essence the Government of the day had, pardon the pun, told the housing industry to "get their house in order" or they would pass legislation to force them to do so in rather draconian ways. This is not dissimilar to how the Government of today act on many issues, self-regulation is often more pressing than that lead by legislation. Let's face it the Solicitors Regulation Authority seem to hold solicitors to a far higher standard than general legislation deems although that is a story for another tome not this one.

NHBRC developed a set of building standards and carried out assessments of the work by their members to help ensure compliance with these standards. Over time a two-year warranty by the builder was administered by the NHBRC and in 1965 this evolved in to the ten-year Buildmark warranty which is what is offered by most providers today.

However as you will see later on in this chapter the two year period is still relevant.

In 1973 the organisation was renamed National House-Building Council (NHBC) and in 1978 it became an insurance company to deliver the Buildmark Warranty itself. It was and remains independent of the House builder and Government. A decade later the current format of the Buildmark warranty was launched albeit it has evolved as you will see below.

In 1985 the then Government introduced legislation that allowed private sector Approved Inspectors (AI) to monitor compliance with Building Regulations. This was quite revolutionary to devolve power over something so important to private companies. The NHBC was the only AI permitted to provide Building Control services for new homes at that time. This was quite a major step because it allowed NHBC to expand its service and took something that had remained in the purview of just the Local Authority away from the Council. This was part and parcel of the reforms that Mrs Thatcher as Prime Minister at the time wished to pass. NHBC being able to carry out building control at the same time as issuing a new homes warranty was a major time saving for the developer.

In 1989 Local Authority Building Control (LABC) looked to launch a ten year warranty to help them compete with the NHBC's move in to the Building Control market. LABC approached the Local Government insurer, Municipal Mutual Insurance (MMI), and a new era in structural home warranties was born. Foundation 15, a fifteen year warranty was launched by MMI. This was the first competition to NHBC's provision of new home warranties. The NHBC responded with 12-year policies for social housing projects. As you can gather this competition lead both providers at the time to increase their offering. No bad thing.

1993 saw Zurich, one of the world's largest and most respected insurers, buy MMI's assets and re-branded and launched its own range of ten year warranties. Zurich innovated with different types of warranty policy for the private sector, the public sector, commercial developments and self-build projects. Cover provided became more flexible with optional additional clauses and 12-year policies where social housing building contracts were under seal.

In the early 1990s a new warranty provider joined the marketplace called Housing Associations Property Mutual (HAPM) offering a warranty purely for social housing projects but with cover which varied in length depending on the element of the building being insured. The load bearing structure could now be insured for up to 35 years. The continual pressure on cost reduction in the social housing sector meant that 35-year cover was no longer affordable and the warranty market was back to the original ten years. HAPM left the market altogether within a few years. This is no surprise, why offer more than is really needed, 35 years was pretty lengthy.

In 1997 an insurance broker called MD Insurance Services launched a brand called Premier Guarantee to offer a ten-year structural warranty in substantially similar format to that of NHBC. Premier Guarantee continue to offer their Buildmark new home warranty policy. This is the most similar to NHBC and I would say that it is rapidly catching up with NHBC in terms of the number of developers that are using the same. Given the fact that Premier can undertake building control as well this makes it attractive to developers from a speed perspective. It also tends to be more competitively priced than NHBC.

During 1999 BLP (Building Life Plans) launched their own insurance policies, similar to those new home warranties offered by other market participants but BLP's insurance policies do not always offer the same type of cover as other new home warranties available. I will look at some of the nuances of various policies below

Zurich shocked the industry in 2009 with its announcement to exit the market completely and it closed its doors to new business at the end of September that year. I always liked the Zurich warranty as it was easy to complete. However many firms fell into a trap of thinking that Zurich provided building control which they did not. In addition the biggest issue for Zurich was that they did not arrange in general, an inspection of the property before cover was issued. The same was true of NHBC as well in the past. Cover could be issued by an unscrupulous developer when the property was not complete.

Other supplies of new home structural warranties are Checkmate, Build zone, One Guarantee, Build safe, ICW and many many others. All are insurance backed albeit this caused issues around 2017 and 2018 when a warranty provider called CRL was backed by two different insurance companies but one insurer went into liquidation. Some policies by CRL were honoured and some were not. Most owners who had a CRL backed policy were offered a refund by the insurance company for them to obtain alternative insurance.

Now I realise you will be asking how could they obtain a structural warranty after the property has been constructed? Believe it or not it is possible to obtain retrospective insurance to cover lack of a structural warranty. If you are acting for a buyer and there is no new homes warranty certificate in place then it is possible to obtain legal indemnity insurance, usually to cover the lender only. At the time of writing I have found several companies who will offer cover for £250,000.00 worth of cover for under £300.00 as a one off premium. Perhaps this shows how much legal indemnity insurance providers value structural warranties.

So I have given you a history of how new homes warranties came into place but this is not the 1930's. Society is now allegedly far more knowledgeable, at least they have the internet to try and convince them that they are. If there were issues with the build of a property the same would be exposed by some investigative journalist. In fact in the past few years most if not all of the major developers have been subject to intense media scrutiny over the build of their properties. All of those properties had a new homes warranty and building control sign off so why is a new homes warranty still relevant today.

Well it is worth pointing out one of the benefits of most new homes warranties that is never spoken of. Most new build developers, as identified in a previous chapter, require people to exchange contracts well before the property is constructed. That means that they are handing over a large sum of money (usually between five (5%) to ten (10%) percent of the purchase price to the developer, sometimes before even a brick is laid. There is an element risk here that the developer will not do what they have been paid to do.

This is where the new homes warranty comes to the buyer's assistance. It offers a level of insurance to guarantee that deposit until the property is constructed. Now I hear you cry "that is wonderful" why am I not told about this? Well a little like how using the new car analogy the sales person will tell you all about the various wonderful gizmos on your new vehicle and will pay a fleeting mention to the air bags that are fitted as standard. No one likes potential issues being highlighted to them. Why? That is because they then become the focus. A developer does not want a buyer to think that they might lose their deposit.

The mind set of someone who thinks they are taking a risk is generally to limited their exposure. Perhaps the buyer might not want to exchange as quickly, as established earlier this is the life blood to a developer, exchanges make things happen so an exchange must happen so nothing must stop it. Perhaps a buyer might try to offer a lesser deposit, again for certain developers, certainly smaller ones they cannot survive without that deposit being available to use towards the purchase of the site.

The main drivers as to why a new-homes warranty though are two-fold, the Consumer Code of New Homes (which we will look at in the chapter creatively named after the same) and mortgage lenders. The UK finance Mortgage Lenders Handbook for Conveyancers (trips of the tongue does it not!) require a new homes warranty. Those familiar with the handbook (and all conveyancers reading this book better be) will know that of course there are subtle differences between the lenders. For example some will accept certain warranties and some will not. Clearly not all uniformity for lenders can be achieved. Having said that if they were all the same it would be boring.

Mortgage lenders require a new homes warranty certificate to be in place to protect their interest as much as the buyers. This is set out at section 6.7 of the Handbook. Although they will also accept something else known as a Professional Consultant's certificate.

Now I hear what is a Professional Consultant's certificate? You may have heard of them by what Estate agents tend to call them, an "Architects Certificate".

Lenders will generally only lend on a newly built, converted or renovated property where the property is covered by a warranty scheme or a Professional Consultant's Certificate (PCC). The PCC is for use by professional consultants when designing and/or monitoring the construction or conversion of residential buildings.

The purpose of the PCC is to confirm to the lender or its conveyancer that a professional consultant:

- has visited the property during construction to check its progress, its strict agreement with drawings approved under building regulations and its conformity with drawings/instructions issued under the building contract;

- will remain liable to the first purchasers and their lender and subsequent purchasers and lenders for the period of six (6) years from the date of the certificate;

- has appropriate experience in the design and/or monitoring of the construction and conversion of residential buildings; and

- will keep a certain level of professional indemnity insurance in force to cover their liabilities under the certificate.

For the purpose of the PCC, a professional consultant must belong to one of the professional bodies listed in section 6.7.4 of the UK Finance Mortgage Lenders' Handbook England and Wales.

This list consists of surveyors, structural engineers, building engineers architects and civil engineers. They must be able to issue a PCC at completion of the property for either the great of the value of the property or two hundred and fifty thousand pounds (£250,000.00) if employed directly by the borrower or in any other case five hundred thousand pounds (£500,000.00). Sometimes a lender will require a collateral warranty from the professional consultant but the lender will specifically state the same in their instructions.

Now you will have seen the big difference between a PCC and a more traditional new homes warranty is that it is limited to six (6) years as opposed to ten (10) years. Some consider this to be the weakest of all the options when it comes to a new homes warranty. However there is a school of thought that conversely believes this to be the strongest form of warranty on offer.

How I hear your minds saying? Well let me enlighten you. The large warranty providers cover thousands of properties across the country. Certain large developers have certain types of homes they build no matter if they are in Hull, Whitehaven, Cardiff, Norwich or Penzance. A PCC will usually only be against a smaller bespoke property. That may suggest that more care is taken with the same and more detail spent on the build.

In addition a large warranty providers has millions at its' disposal to cover any claims or issues. The sole architect who is signing a PCC is placing their livelihood on the line if they get it wrong. Do they want to make their spouse and children homeless by signing off on something they should not have done.

I am not saying that one is better than another as there are arguments for both and I just want to make you the reader consider the same. I shall leave you to make your own mind up to see which you think may be better. More importantly now that you are aware of the same you can perhaps make these arguments to your clients so they can make their own decisions more fully informed because of your careful message regarding the same.

So we have looked at the warranties and an alternative as well as the history of the same. So what actually do they do? Well as they sound, they are structural warranties to protect the buyer against structural defects.

Once the property is built, the warranty is split into two periods – the defects insurance period, which covers the first two (2) years, and the structural insurance period which covers years three (3) to ten (10).

During the first two years in the home, if there are issues with the work the developer has done, such as the windows letting in rain because they're not sealed properly or the heating not working because the pipes are somehow defective, the developer is obliged to return, investigate and attempt to remedy the same.

During the structural insurance period, the developer is only responsible for major problems with the structure of the house. This includes foundations, the external render, roofs, ceilings, chimneys and load-bearing parts of the floors.

Smaller 'defects' are the responsibility of the owner, including non-structural defects such as problems with their gutters or fixtures and fittings. The developer will not be attending for damage caused by wear and tear of actually living in the property. Buyers have on occasion I know called a developer and asked them to attend the property for a major defect only to find it was to change a light bulb in a bedroom.

Buyers should be keenly made aware of the fact that the first two (2) years of warranty cover falls within the remit of the builder so they do not miss the end of that period. In fairness most of the major developer are very good at making sure that the buyer is fully aware of the same.

Understandably, natural wear and tear is not covered by a new home warranty, neither is weather damage or any problems resulting from the owner not maintaining the property adequately. I have seen incidences of damp being caused at a property because the owners have never actually ventilated their property during their period of ownership. As my dear Mother is fond of saying, "there is nowt so queer as folk".

As all warranty providers are insurers, it is worth remembering that they may not always be as willing to carry out (and pay for!) remedial work. As is always the case with insurance, the small print is key. Now please do not take this as me trying to be on some sort of crusade about insurance in general. It serves a worthwhile important function in our society but too many people abuse it which results in higher premiums for the rest of us. Rant over.

I always point out to my clients that I tell them to make sure they contact the developer as soon as possible. Keep a record of all communication including dates and times of telephone calls. This will be needed if there are problems with getting your developer to address the issue.

Both the LABC and Premier Guarantee warranty policies have a one thousand (£1,000.00) pound excess. This means the home owner will pay the first one thousand (£1,000.00) of each claim made under the warranty. Each provider has slightly different rules so it is worth each buyer checking the same once they have had the warranty documents.

The providers of warranties in the UK all adhere to the Consumer Code for Homebuilders. The code features a dispute resolution scheme which can be used during the first two (2) years if the develoepr will not carry out the necessary remedial work.

Remember, the builder will only be liable for problems detailed in the contract. I would always advise buyers to make sure there is a "snagging" provision to allow you to get little issues sorted – such as doors catching on carpets – directly with the developer. Most developers no longer refer to a snagging inspection but call the same a "new home tour". For starters it sounds better and quite frankly the level of detail that most developers go to now to ensure that the property is immaculate is pretty impressive. A term often heard is "sparkle clean" where the developer has the property thoroughly cleaned even after it has had a level of cleaning already carried out so it is perfect.

If the first owner sells, the warranty is transferred to the buyer of that property. It used to be that a formal assignment need to take place. This is no longer necessary. Any work the owners have done on their home – such as loft extensions or conservatories – will not be covered by the warranty. It is worth mentioning that if you are acting for someone who is buying a new home from a previous owner that the company warranties supplied for such works are not always transferrable. In other words, if the seller had a conservatory installed with a ten-year guarantee from the installation firm, when they sell the house to the new owner, the guarantee often becomes invalid.

So what should a buyer's conveyancer really be considering when reporting on a new homes warranty? It is not as if they can change it for the buyer is it?

Well I think for starters it is worth checking that the buyer's mortgage lender will accept the warranty. Given that there are so many warranty providers the need to check that the buyer's chosen lender will cover the same is key. If they don't then the simple fact remains that the seller will not change the same. Why should they when they have spent thousands on the same. It may be that the lender will take a view on an individual case so that should be reported to them but it is important to check if the warranty is acceptable or not.

Personally once that issue is addressed I think it would be prudent to explain to the buyer what the warranty will and will not cover briefly. You should certainly point them to the warranty providers website which will always have a lot more detail on the warranty itself. The fact that they are all slightly different will save the conveyancer the issue of trying to reinvent the wheel on each report they have to do.

In addition I think it would be sensible also to ascertain who will be carrying out the building control function for this property. If it is the warranty provider then great you know that they will do the same around the same time. If not you will need to make a note to check that building control will follow and from who.

This can be a bone of contention with buyers. Many times over the years I have been told "I don't know what the delay is because the property is complete". Yes it may be constructed but that does not mean that everything that is needed to live in the same, bathroom and kitchen to name some obvious items, are installed and working. Quite often a property can be constructed but not connected to the services. As I always like to say with new build property, particularly on acquisition of sites, it is what you cannot see that is likely to cause the issues.

Most of all I think a buyer's conveyancer should make the following clear to their client. A new homes structural warranty is not a magical cure for all problems. Just like the warranty on a car it will not cover everything just the major items. Therefore just like the brake pads on a car are not covered, particularly when you race up to a roundabout then hammer on the anchors to avoid going on to the same, wear and tear around the home is not covered either.

Well that is new homes warranties covered I believe now we will go onto the next chapter where we will discuss searches and the situations where search indemnity insurance may seem a more suitable option in respect of timeframe and economic value.

CHAPTER FIVE

SEARCHES

Paul Sams

So searches? Conveyancers find comfort in them do they not? Commercial Property Lawyers like to cuddle their CPSE 1 enquiries, or as I like to call them the "not applicable form" as most answers are no or not applicable to the questions. Conveyancers love searches. They must have them must they not? Agents and clients ask for them and lender must have them. Well with new build there needs to be some reality checks. Hopefully I can provide them in this chapter.

We do searches because lenders want a local search to protect them. The UK Finance mortgage lenders handbook sets out exactly what they want to see at 5.4 and 5.5 which I set out here:

5.4 Searches and Reports

5.4.1 In carrying out your investigation, you must ensure that all usual and necessary searches and enquiries have been carried out. You must report any adverse entry to us but we do not want to be sent the search itself. We must be named as the applicant in the Land Registry search.

5.4.2 In addition, you must ensure that any other searches which may be appropriate to the particular property, taking into account its locality and other features are carried out.

5.4.3 All searches except where there is a priority period must not be more than six months old at completion.

5.4.4 You must advise us of any contaminated land entries revealed in the local authority search. Check part 2 to see if we want to receive environmental or contaminated land reports (as opposed to contaminated land entries revealed in the local authority search). If we do not, you do not need to make these enquiries on our behalf.

5.4.5 Check part 2 to see if we accept personal searches.

5.4.6 Check part 2 to see if we accept search insurance.

5.4.7 If we accept personal searches or search insurance you must ensure that:-

- a suitably qualified search agent carries out the personal search and has indemnity insurance that adequately protects us; or

- the search insurance policy adequately protects us.

5.4.8 You are satisfied that you will be able to certify that the title is good and marketable unless stated otherwise in our specific requirements listed in part 2.

5.5 Planning and Building Regulations

5.5.1 You must by making appropriate searches and enquiries take all reasonable steps (including any further enquiries to clarify any issues which may arise) to ensure:

- the property has the benefit of any necessary planning consents (including listed building consent) and building regulation approval for its construction and any subsequent change to the property and its current use; and

- there is no evidence of any breach of the conditions of that or any other consent or certificate affecting the property; and
- that no matter is revealed which would preclude the property from being used as a residential property or that the property may be the subject of enforcement action.

If there is evidence of such a breach or matter but in your professional judgment there is no reasonable prospect of enforcement action and, following reasonable enquiries, you are satisfied that the title is good and marketable and you can provide an unqualified certificate of title, we will not insist on indemnity insurance and you may proceed.

5.5.2 If there is such evidence and all outstanding conditions will not be satisfied by completion, where you are not able to provide an unqualified certificate of title, you should report this to us in accordance with 2.3.

5.5.3 Check part 2 to see if copies of planning permissions, building regulations and other consents or certificates should be sent to us.

5.5.4 If the property will be subject to any enforceable restrictions, for example under an agreement (such as an agreement under section 106 of the Town and Country Planning Act 1990) or in a planning permission, which, at the time of completion, might reasonably be expected materially to affect its value or its future marketability, you should report this to us (see part 2).

As you can clearly see it sets out that you must do at least seventeen searches that your search provider has recommended? Actually it does not. The only search that a lender really wants you to do is a local search. I know that this may make conveyancers reading this keel over in shock but honestly that is all you have to do.

Now the reality is that we tend to do more searches than that. Personally I like to do a local, drainage, environmental and planning search. I insure against chancel insurance as it is easier. If it were in my motherland of the Northeast or other areas with various mining issues I would carry out the appropriate mining search.

On a new build though I favour search insurance if the lender will accept it. Why I hear you ask? Well for starters we are in a race to get it through quickly most of the time so search insurance removes the delay of waiting for a search. It can take months in certain areas for the same to come through.

Mainly though I favour search insurance because the planning history a lender wants us to confirm is before us. The seller will provide it. We do not care if there was a caravan on the site before. What we want to know is what there is now has planning consent. Well we know that because the seller has provided it. They will also probably provide confirmation that it has been built or will be in accordance with planning. The Help to Buy scheme insists on that being the case.

I understand the need to do a search on a second-hand property. Owners like to tinker with their properties so they may have added an extension. It is nice to see they have building control sign off, not so nice to find out it does not exist but at least you know. On a new property it will not have an extension or should I say it should not have one as a new property!

Having all that information encourages me to be confident in using search insurance as it saves the time and cost of a search plus makes it a more streamlined process. Now some of you reading this will be thinking, what about the other searches?

Well let us have a look at them. A drainage search confirms if the property is connected to mains drainage. For that to be confirmed the property needs to be established. As it is being built or if it has been built the water board will not be able to tell if it is connected or not. Give them a chance to update their records. I therefore think a drainage search is a waste of time and money.

The same applies to an environmental search. Whatever is being constructed will have to have had planning. To have planning various consents and enquiries have to be sought of the local authority. Many of these are in relation to environmental issues. You will find that any information the seller has provided to the local authority, which they will provide to you as the buyer's solicitors, will be far more detailed and useful than an environmental search. All I would say is that it will not say pass or fail on the front of it!

Turning to planning searches, well I would expect the planning search would show that lots of building was going on nearby as in most cases the property you will be acting upon will be on a larger estate. I have had clients demand I carry out a planning search before on a new build site which I have done as instructed to find them shocked that other houses are being built nearby. Always brings a wry smile to my face.

So searches. If you have to do them then do them but do not be blinded into thinking you have to do all of the time. A conveyancer should be experienced enough to use their experience to know what a search should be used, because the lender or buyer insists or that alternatives are available. Speaking of mortgages that brings us conveniently on to that topic so I will pass you over to Miss East to educate you on some of the issues over the same.

CHAPTER SIX

MORTGAGES

Rebecca East

It may sound obvious but one of the most important steps before the conveyancing process can even begin (and more often than not, before an offer would even be accepted by a Developer) is to make sure that your client has their finances in order. Most developers will require sight of an agreement in principle from a lender first and foremost, but this does not necessarily mean your client can secure their mortgage finance.

Whilst the process involved in respect of a mortgage for the purchase of a new build property may not seem too dissimilar to the process involved with a second-hand property purchase, there are in fact various factors that have an effect on completion and therefore on the mortgage. Developers will of course have to rely on things such as supply of materials, weather conditions and availability of having the property signed off as structurally sound before legal completion. All of these stages can have an effect on whether a mortgage offer needs to be extended. You want to first check the reservation form to see if you're given an anticipated build date as this may require your client to obtain a mortgage offer extension or having to reapply for a new product and thus offer before they even have their first mortgage offer. Lenders therefore need to know from the outset that your client is purchasing a new build property (this is usually dealt with by the mortgage broker or lender upon application however) as your client will likely need a mortgage product that will allow for a delay between exchange and completion.

Aside from build date, one of the first questions to ask clients upon receiving the reservation form is whether they have started engaging their lender or mortgage broker to submit their mortgage application. This tends on average to be the sticking point with new build conveyancing matters so we always want to ensure this is submitted at the earliest possible opportunity to prevent delays with being in a position to exchange contracts.

As part of the mortgage application process the mortgage lender will arrange for a surveyor to carry out a valuation survey to ensure the property being purchased is worth the funds that are being loaned. If your client is buying off-plan, the valuation will be based on the plans and specification the developer has provided. If the property is built and ready for occupation, the surveyor will need to visit the property to carry this out. Whilst you will have no control over arranging for this to be done as soon as possible (and I quote in Mr Sams's words *"SECONDS AND YOUR DEAD"*) so even if the valuation has not yet been carried out and no mortgage offer has been issued, it will somehow still be your fault. You can only control the controllable so at this stage ensure you have your ducks in a row for the things you can control and the rest will fall into place.

The UK Finance Mortgage Lenders' Handbook should be deemed the conveyancing bible when it comes to checking lender requirements on a specific matter. It is unlikely that a week will go by where this is not checked. If you find yourself thinking *"I haven't checked that for a while..."* put the book down and go and check it as it is updated constantly, daily in fact, so you cannot rely on the fact you checked X requirement last week so it must still be ok. This handbook has been adopted by most lenders now and contains the standardised instructions from lenders to conveyancing lawyers.

The handbook is divided into three parts. Part 1 sets out the guidance and main instructions to be disclosed by conveyancing lawyers to the lender. Part 2 sets out lenders' specific requirements which arise from instructions. Part 3 is applicable in those circumstances where a conveyancing practitioner is acting solely for the lender in a residential conveyancing transaction.

On 1st January 2010 the Building Societies Association (BSA) introduced a new set of standardised instructions to be used in situations involving members of the BSA. The reason for this is that BSA members wanted to remain independent from the UK Finance Mortgage Lenders' handbook but they still had the requirement for having a set of standardised instructions available to lawyers.

Whilst the majority of mortgage lenders accept search indemnity insurance (see chapter 5), it is important to find out early on which lender your client is likely to sway towards using so you can be prepared to check the UK Finance Handbook for that lender's requirements on searches. If your client is looking to use a lender who does not accept insurance and requires searches to be carried out, you want to make sure searches are submitted as soon as instructions are returned from your client. I would always recommend advising your client to pay for an official local search as they are on average returned much faster than a regulated search. Yes they are more expensive but in the grand scheme of things I doubt approximately £60 is really going to break the bank and I doubt a client would say no. Time is money.

It may seem like I'm teaching you to suck eggs here but clients and developers want to exchange and complete as soon as possible and anything in the way of that is deemed a nuisance (even if it is not in your control such as searches being returned or mortgage offer being issued).

The deadline for exchange of contracts is usually 4 weeks from receipt of draft documents by the developers' solicitor or from the date the reservation was placed by your client. From the moment that reservation form is received in your inbox the exchange deadline clock is ticking. . You should have an instant checklist (physical or metaphorical) of things you need to look out for and potentially check the UK Finance Handbook for lenders requirements. These include but are not limited to;

- Gifts
- Incentives
- Rent Charges (if applicable)
- Occupiers
- If Leasehold – what are the ground rent provisions? Are these acceptable to my client's lender?

For the purposes of this chapter I will mainly be discussing gifts and incentives. Paul will seek to explore Rent Charges in chapter 8. My advice on the other points would be to check the mortgage offer, check the handbook and if you're still unsure, refer to lender for authority to proceed.

Even if you think you know the lenders handbook like the back of your hand, it is always worth checking. Takes a minute to do but better to be safe than sorry given the constant updates lenders make to try and catch us as conveyancing lawyers out.

In respect of gifted deposits, this should form part of your initial client due diligence checks. Essentially you need to be asking your clients the question early on. There is nothing worse than getting to report stage when you find out the "savings" your client told you they had built up themselves through their own earnings transpires to be a cash lump sum from Dad a few weeks ago. We are encountering gifted deposits from the bank of Mum and Dad (and more commonly Grandparents now too) more and more often and whilst clients should be declaring this during their mortgage application (and our initial due diligence checks), this isn't always the case.

I have recently had a handful of cases where even though the clients have said to me that they declared this to their lender, there was no such mention in the mortgage offer and upon checking the UK Finance Handbook that particular lender requests we refer this back to them for approval. You can easily be waiting 3-5 working days (if you're lucky!) for a response from some lenders in connection with this approval so as I said – ask the question early to ensure it's not something you find yourself having to declare to lender weeks down the line. If you do have to declare this, please get a fax number or an email address to send approval to. Even if it means sitting on the phone to a lender to obtain this information, it will save you time in the long run. Snail mail will not be appreciated by clients and developers and they will insist you call the lender at least fourteen times a day to request a response.

Many developers offer incentives or freebies to tempt buyers to purchase a new build property. These can include having your clients Stamp Duty paid, moving costs paid and legal fees paid to name a few. Almost every new build purchase I've dealt with has had incentives with the majority being cash incentives. I do always wonder how a developer hands these incentives out. Is it a case of negotiation or does it depend where in the financial year it is? Anyway, I digress – it is again important to first check the Disclosure of Incentives form, check with your client they have agreed to the same and then cross reference this with your mortgage offer. Incentives can affect the amount a client can borrow.

A mortgage broker will be able to advise on the potential impact of buyer incentives on your client's mortgage application. Lenders are including these in their offers now (albeit not always) so check the position as to whether you need to refer this to the lender for approval. Santander for instance, I know that they are happy to proceed without us reporting the incentives to them provided we can comply with the following *"The Conveyancer does not need to report sales incentives to us if the seller is a developer and the incentive is a cash incentive not exceeding 5% of the purchase price and/or payment of legal fees and/or stamp duty land tax in respect of the purchase."*

Goes without saying that the conveyancing practitioner is obliged to check the mortgage offer to ensure that the information contained therein is correct and to report any inaccuracies to the lender. These inaccuracies include checking address of property, purchase price and clients' full names. These seem to be the main issues that arise day to day. You will also need to check the requirements and special conditions contained in the mortgage offer. Towards the end of a mortgage offer there will often be a list of special conditions. Some conditions are directed specifically at the borrower but some are for the conveyancing practitioner to deal with or at least be able to satisfy prior to completion.

These conditions cover a multitude of different subjects such as ensuring existing debts and credit cards are repaid on or before completion, requirement for buildings insurance from completion, requirement for life insurance to be in place for the borrowers from completion and confirming the gifted deposit (if applicable) is given freely. Some lenders will require you to confirm the position before completion whereas other lenders will assume upon submitting the certificate of title (COT) that you have satisfied these conditions. It is definitely something to look out for as there is nothing worse than receiving a call or email from a lender a few days before completion confirming you have not satisfied specific requirement. Some lenders such as Bank of Ireland and Precise (to name a few) are very on the ball when it comes to special conditions and will not accept your COT until these are satisfied.

The Developer's solicitor will confirm whether completion will be given by way of fixed completion date or on notice. With completion on notice you will not be given a completion date to work towards but instead will be given a certain number of days' notice of a completion date in order than you may prepare your file. You will however be given a rough idea of the anticipated build date and longstop provision for insertion into the contract but the date specifically will be unknown until the property has been deemed structurally sound. Why does that effect your clients' mortgage I hear you ask? The mortgage expiry date contained in all mortgage offers needs to be taken into consideration when agreeing completion on notice. Most developers will give you an anticipated build date or anticipated legal completion date (ALCD) that can be anywhere upwards of 2-3 months in advance of exchange. With most mortgage offers being issued with an expiry date 3-6 months from the date of issue, you need to check that your clients are aware before exchange of the ALCD and longstop in case they need to re-submit their mortgage application or request via their mortgage broker for an extension of their existing mortgage offer. Whilst most clients will be fine with this at the time (yet will later make a point of saying they weren't aware of this when the completion date is delayed because of the build suffering delays!) you need to ensure your client is prepared to re-submit their mortgage application if necessary and that they are aware that if they are made redundant, change jobs, take out a new finance agreement etc this can affect their ability to secure the same product and deal they had before.

To ensure your clients position in protected you could see if the developer's solicitor would agree to the insertion of a safety net clause i.e. if the clients cannot obtain a new or extended mortgage offer that they can rescind the contractual agreement to purchase the property and have refunded their deposit. Other developers may instead agree a longstop date being inserted into the contract that is before the expiry of your client's mortgage offer. Whilst these options are not conclusive, you certainly want to have this to the forefront of your mind before exchange to make sure no issues arise in respect of this down the road.

Once you have exchanged contracts and have a fixed completion date or you've been served notice to complete and now have a completion date you will need to submit your certificate of title (COT) to your clients' lender. The certificate of title (sometimes called the Report on Title) is a certificate given to the lender to confirm that the title is a good an marketable title and that the lenders' instructions, contained in the mortgage offer and in the UK Finance handbook, have been complied with. As some lenders require several days' notice of draw-down of funds, this should be submitted to the lender in good time for completion. From personal experience you can get funds drawn-down much faster than the allocated 5 working days' notice as must lenders require but this does not take away from the requirement to submit this as soon as possible to prevent delays. You will need to check to see if there is a requirement for re-inspection and if there is such requirement, that this is carried out as soon as possible to prevent delays with completion.

As with second-hand property purchases, on completion you will need to ensure you have clear bankruptcy search for all borrowers as well as giftors. By submitting a certificate of title (and using mortgage funds on completion) you are providing confirmation that the borrowers are not bankrupt and that there are no insolvency proceedings against them. Pending completion we would hold the mortgage advance on trust for the lender and therefore we must comply with the lender's instructions. Non-compliance of these instructions will constitute a breach of trust.

Together with clear bankruptcy search you will also need to ensure you have suitable priority search in place. It is likely that with this being a new build property you will need to submit an official search with priority of part (OS2). This search is used when the subject property forms part of a larger title (as with most new build properties). Whilst submission of the OS2 is akin to that of an official search of whole with priority (OS1), the result for an OS2 is not returned instantly so you want to ensure you submit your priority search in good time for completion to ensure you have a clear result on or before the day of completion. Once the result is returned you want to make sure there are no adverse entries revealed and that this priority remains in place and in date until you are ready to submit the HM Land Registry application to change the register after completion. Lenders are frequently trying to find reason to kick solicitor firms off their panel so you want to make sure this is in place on completion and until such time the registration is submitted.

Well that's the end of the mortgages chapter. I hope this chapter has given you the necessary practical and vital knowledge of what to specifically look out for when reporting to your client on their mortgage offer. Whilst there are not massive differences between the mortgage offers of second-hand market property purchases and that of new build transactions, the slight differences explored above can mean the difference between meeting the exchange deadline and being responsible for unnecessary delays because something wasn't picked up on first glance. I will now hand you back over to Paul who will discuss the very hand in hand topic when discussing new build conveyancing and that is the Help to Buy Scheme.

CHAPTER SEVEN

HELP TO BUY

Paul Sams

One of the biggest differences to dealing with new build properties compared to resale properties is the use of the Help to Buy scheme. Within this chapter we will have a look at the history of shared equity schemes, how the Help to Buy scheme has worked, the new scheme from 2021 onwards as well as how the loan has to be repaid. Yes, before you say it I know that Help to Buy ends in 2023 but see what I say at the end of this chapter why I believe it will still be relevant for years to come.

Firstly I should determine here and now that in this chapter when I say Help to Buy I am referring to the equity loan scheme. I do not propose to comment on the Help to Buy ISA (much) or the shared ownership element of Help to Buy. This chapter is dedicated to the shared equity loan only available for new property.

Just briefly, I am glad that the Help to Buy ISA scheme has ended. I was becoming like the "bad news bear" in relation to the same. By this I mean that clients would reveal they had a HTB ISA and I would be the one giving them the bad news that they could not claim the HTB ISA bonus monies as they were buying for more than two hundred and fifty thousand (£250,000.00) outside of London. It seems that the ISA providers were poor at communicating this to their savers and it was left to me to break this news to the buyer. In some cases this really threw the buyers into turmoil as they were counting on those funds once they had purchased the property. The fact that the bonus could not be used towards the deposit or purchase price did not help either. I for one am glad it has closed to be in a way be replaced by the Life time ISA (L-ISA) scheme which appears to be a fairer way to assist buyers as well as being a useful way to save.

Now I have finished my soap box moment about the Help to Buy ISA scheme I think it is fair to give you an idea of how the Help to Buy equity loan scheme came into being. This may be a shock to many of you but this is certainly not the first Government backed scheme to assist with the purchase of new homes. In fact it is the latest in a long line of Government backed schemes to assist with the purchase of new homes. You will see at the end of this chapter why I do not think it will be the last either.

You may ask why new homes only? Well mainly because housing is such a good income driver for taxes in this Country. For every new home sold it is thought/claimed that ten thousand (£10,000.00) pounds is generated for the wider economy which in turns raises more revenue for the Government. The figure is much lower for the sale of a property that already exists. Since the change in the 1980's of not so many properties being constructed by local authorities the need to drive housing in the private sector is much more pressured from central Government.

The above is not a political statement merely one of fact. Social housing provides a vital role in our society. However I would lie if I did not say that often clients when purchasing ask where the social housing units are on a new estate or whether they will contribute the same amount to the estate charge that inevitably seems to be charged on new properties. Handily there is a chapter on this later on in the book.

There have been many schemes in the past similar to Help to Buy but none have captured the attention as much as Help to Buy has. I shall explain my cynical thoughts on why later in this chapter. However equity sharing schemes have been around for decades. In a way equity loans are akin to shared ownership without the paraphernalia and dare I say it, trepidation that seems to accompany the same for some reason. Long may that fear continue I say as it keeps Mrs Sams employed as a leading expert in that field!

In the past there have been equity loans for key workers. Now in the time of the pandemic that phrase has been thrown around a lot but in reality it related at the time of key worker loans to those who would always be considered key workers. That being those in the NHS, those in the Police Force and Fire Service. The same was extended to those in key services as well. For instance I remember years ago having a client obtain a key worker equity loan when they worked for one of the ferry companies that transported people plus goods across to the Isle of Wight. Their role was key because without them those on the Island would be cut off from crucial supplies.

The key worker loan scheme essentially was a simplified equity loan. A sum of ten thousand (£10,000.00) pounds typically could be taken to assist with a house purchase. That sum had to be paid back as a percentage of the eventual sale price in the future or the sum that was loaned in the first place but a defined sum of compound interest. The schemes were limited because funding came from central Government to each Local Council who then had to determine how much they would use and for whom.

Where I am based in Hampshire the key worker loan scheme ran from April 2004 to March 2006. Loans for thirty thousand (£30,000.00) pounds were offered by the local authority. Given the house prices in Hampshire then it was possible on occasion for the right candidate to have a loan of actually fifty thousand (£50,000.00) pounds as opposed to the limit above.

No repayments were required for the loan but an equity charge was placed as second charge against the property. This loan would be expressed as a percentage so that when the property was sold in the future then the percentage had to be repaid. For instance if a keyworker used a keyworker loan to purchase a property for one hundred and fifty thousand (£150,000.00) pounds with a thirty thousand (£30,000.00) equity loan that equity loan would be worth twenty percent (20%) of the property). If the property was sold in the future for say two hundred thousand (£200,00.00) pounds then the equity loan repayment would be forty thousand (£40,000.00) pounds. Simple enough.

Some of the quirks of the key worker loan scheme, aside from the fact that few were offered, included the need for the loan to be repaid if the borrower ended being a key worker or if they changed role within their organisation in certain circumstances. A noble scheme but few people took advantage of the same mainly because so few could either benefit from the scheme and the political decisions involved with giving preferential treatment to a certain group of people.

One of the more successful schemes was the Thames Valley My Choice Home Buy scheme also known as the Metropolitan Housing Trust scheme. An equity loan here could be obtained for up to fifty percent (50%) of the purchase price of a new property. Yes that much could be obtained. Not shared ownership but shared equity secured by way of a second charge.

This scheme proved relatively popular but was most likely marred because it came into being in 2007. 2007 being just before one of the biggest property recessions ever. Prices fell quite rapidly. I recall dealing with a new build block of flats in Southampton with memorably small kitchens. The joke was that the built in over microwave combi oven that each apartment had was just big enough to fit a mouse in to cook. Said one-bedroom apartments with a parking space were selling for around one hundred and twenty-five thousand (£125,000.00) pounds until June 2008. By December of that year I was acting for buyers paying seventy six (£76,000.00) for the same. At the time of writing they are now selling for around £125,000.00 still to this day some fifteen years later.

So shy of the issues caused by this scheme and rapid price drops you would think that would be the end of equity sharing scheme? Oh no, Government came up with a new scheme. Small political comment here, no matter your political persuasion you have to credit both major political parties in the United Kingdom for at least both trying to come up with schemes to assist the new build housing market. Albeit they do seem to rehash the same theme all the time, they at least both try.

The next scheme off the production line from the civil service was the Home Buy direct scheme. This worked on the basis that the parties buying the new property (and remember all these schemes are only for new build properties) had to have a household income under sixty thousand (£60,000.00) combined. The Government and the Developer would both provide a combined equity loan of thirty percent (30%) of the purchase price.

Cynics at the time suggested that if developers actually around that time had stopped building as many city centre developments as they seemed obsessed with, more profit in building up into the sky on a small footprint of a site than building sideways, that such schemes like Home Buy direct would not be needed. I will not criticise the scheme as it provided a living for me.

The scheme had the quirk of both the Government and the developer needing to have a second charge on the title to the property. Of course they had to have a charge each. This resulted in not one second charge but also a third charge plus a deed of priority between the two to say that they were not a second and third charge but equal. Woe betide you though if you registered the charge for the developer before the charge for the Government as the administering Housing Association would take you to task over the same.

This scheme proved relatively popular but had its restrictions. Lenders were happy they were only having to provide mortgages equivalent to sixty five percent (65%) loan to value. However they were wary that developers were trying leverage prices as they did before 2008. I should mention that part of the reason for the fall in house price values in 2008 was due to the way that valuations took place.

Before 2008 surveyors were instructed by lenders to take valuer of a new build property based on the previous few sale prices on a site. The logic was that the market had set the price. If a buyer was prepared to pay that price then another one would pay a similar price. Developers, legitimately I hasten to add, took advantage of this by increasing the prices on a site as they went. They knew the last sale price was key for the surveyor so kept pushing prices up. This in turn resulted in prices across the board rising. Hindsight is a wonderful thing.

Lenders deciding that there was an element of risk in this (what letting the developer control prices!) instructed surveyors from 2008 to not just look at the last sale price on a particular site but also to look for comparables nearby. This took control from a developer. How lenders were concerned about valuations on new property so were cautious about the same. Not all lenders for instance were prepared to lend on properties under Homebuy direct.

Following on from Homebuy direct came Firstbuy. In reality this was a rehashed Homebuy direct scheme but limited to now a twenty percent (20%) equity loan. This would be funded equally between the developer and the Government. The scheme had the annoying quirks for the buyer's solicitors that Homebuy direct had. I forgot to mention earlier the amount of paper that Homebuy direct had involved with it. Firstbuy continued this.

Each of the two charges needed to be registered behind the first charge. Neither charge was approved by HM Land Registry so a separate RX 1 form was needed to add the restriction per charge to the title. In addition to this was the deed of priority for the second and third charge. Not to mention all the paperwork that was needed for the actual lease or transfer. AP 1 forms became attached to quite hefty applications.

Do not forget this was before electronic submissions to HM Land Registry. Mind you it was also before the huge delays that HM Land Registry now seem to have with all new build property. Is all technological advancement progress? I digress.

So Firstbuy came along and we all thought 'here we go again'. The main issue was that the scheme had very limited funding. If there is less money then few people benefit. Due to the high prices in London there was really only enough funding available at the time to help a mere nine hundred (900) first-time buyers on to the market.

After Firstbuy came riding over the hill on a white charger the developer and buyers white knight, Help to Buy. Saviour of the housing market, raising values of everyone's property and helping thousands buy their home.

Help to Buy commenced in 2013. There were two crucial differences in my mind that made it more popular than any previous scheme and I am not talking about the fact that the Government made a huge amount of money available for it. Firstly unlike previous schemes, this was not limited to first-time buyers, those who had homes could use it and secondly from the developers point of view they did not have to put any money into the scheme.

These two important variations opened up the scheme to a whole range of new people on both sides of the equation. I recall acting for a couple in 2013, one of the first Help to Buy loans I was dealing with, who intended to purchase for five hundred thousand pounds (£500,000.00) but when they discovered Help to Buy they purchased for six hundred thousand (£600,000.00). Their rationale was they could buy the bigger house they wanted now rather than waiting.

Developers had before been required to commit funds to the scheme. This tended to be dominated in previous scheme by the bigger developers as they could afford to commit the millions needed to take advantage of the scheme. Now under Help to Buy smaller developers could take advantage of the scheme for a few thousand pounds. A whole new market had opened up. Help to Buy had empowered not just buyers but all developers to be able to take advantage of a scheme that really has driven the market.

I will not criticise the scheme. It has brought many into home ownership and contributed massively to the economy. Personally I have done very well financially from the fees earned acting for buyers who have taken advantage of the scheme. I am though always saddened personally when I see people selling one property with a Help to Buy loan to purchase a new property also with a Help to Buy loan. In my mind that should have been stopped at the outset. To give buyers a helping hand on to the property ladder I am a huge fan of. To help then again, less so.

Help to Buy has been described to me as the "crack cocaine" of the UK property market. The large developers have all seen their sales and share prices flourish because of the scheme. They need to acknowledge this which I think most do. Smaller developers have relied on it too. Many have sold entire sites based on Help to Buy funding. They will need to get used to other ways to make money though as the scheme will end this year in 2023.

Before looking at the new process for Help to Buy (now it seems known as the 2021 to 2023 Help to Buy scheme) it is worth considering the "technicalities" of the Help to Buy scheme as was that is ending at the end of March 2021.

When Help to Buy came into being, the local Help to Buy often asked me to speak to other solicitors and professionals at gatherings to explain how they could speed up the process. Now I have been involved with equity schemes for years and I know, at least I confidently like to think I know, the nuances of the same. Not being conceited but I have spent a lot of time dealing with the same for a long time so am confident in handling the same. It seems that a great deal of my profession are not. In fact some of the horror stories my contacts at the Help to Buy agents have told me over the years I struggle to comprehend as times.

The paperwork used in the Help to Buy scheme was created some time ago. Having seen all the equity sharing second charge schemes referred to above I can confidentially spot the wording. This seems to be the issue for my peers. Lawyers being lawyers they cannot help but have a little "fiddle" with the standard wording. Let us face it and I agree with this in particular to have to say "there are no incentives save for nil" always irritated me. The English language requires us to say "there are no incentives" but "Help to Buy English" requires this nonsense phrase.

I accepted it (reluctantly) many years ago but some conveyancers still refuse to accept the same and want to argue over the same. Good for them but they will not win. Every "t" must be crossed and every dot made just so to comply with the scheme. The Help to Buy agents are punished by Homes England if the scheme is not followed as Homes England have set out so why or more importantly how can they argue over the same? Do as they say and you will get your authority to exchange, do not and you will not. It is that simple.

Many conveyancers I speak to tell me they won't deal with Help to Buy. Well that is nice but very limiting and to be frank always makes me smirk. The scheme is not hard to understand. Let me start with the basics and then move on to the changes of the latest scheme.

Under the Help to Buy scheme as a whole, the developer registers themselves and a site for the scheme. Once they have confirmation they can offer Help to Buy to buyers. The buyer once they have applied for the scheme, usually handled by their mortgage broker. The Help to Buy agent, if happy with all the paperwork, will issue the following, an Authority to proceed, a personal worked example and a copy equity deed. The new 2021-2023 scheme will also have first-time buyer declarations and a direct debit mandate. I should point out now that the scheme moving forwards will only be for first-time buyers, more on that later.

Turning to the authority to proceed this is a simple document which sets out the details of the property, parties involved, figures involved including the equity loan sum, the mortgage sum and the sum being provided by the buyer towards the purchase price. The personal worked example is an illustrative guide to the buyer of what they may have to pay back as interest after the first five years of the scheme which is interest free. It also gives information based on potential sale prices to show how much may need to be paid back in the future. Whether buyers pay attention to this I am not sure!

The equity deed is a mortgage deed the buyer has to sign as they would any other mortgage deed. A buyer's conveyancer has certain obligations under the scheme that they need to follow when acting under the scheme which includes how they report to the buyer on these documents. Personally I always send these to my client as soon as possible with a report letter. This is separate to my report on legal title or mortgage as I believe it is important for the buyer to have this separately. I call this letter the "Panorama defence". This is because I have this fear that buyers will always turn around and say "Mr Sams never told me that" and I have no desire to be on the BBC one evening in the future having to justify what I did or did not do years ago. I therefore send a detailed report letter with each Help to Buy deed plus the other documents of which I ask the buyers to sign then return one copy. No harm in being careful.

A buyer must be sent a copy of the authority to proceed and personal worked example by their conveyancer. Under the latest version of the scheme a first-time buyer declaration must be sent to each buyer and as a conveyancer under the scheme we have to advise on the same. It is our role here to make it clear that if they lie it is fraud.

This point always reminds me of a tale told to me by a developer a few years ago. On the day of completion the husband had an attack on his conscious and told his wife plus selling developer (as well as I presume his) conveyancer that although he had said he was not named on the title to another property he might be with his former partner. Furthermore she was not really his former partner but she was actually his former wife. In fact she was still his wife because he never got around to divorcing her. One has to admire the fact that he felt that he could become a bigamist but that he was not prepared to defraud Homes England. I am sure they are pleased to know the power they have.

Now turning to the advice a conveyancer has to give to a buyer under the scheme this must cover the following documents:

- The Help to Buy Buyers' Guide – they should have already been sent a copy but I always send a link to a further copy as well as covering the main points – more below on that

- The Personal Worked example and the role plus contact details of the Help to Buy Agent

- The First-time buyer's declaration

- The Authority to Proceed

- The Equity mortgage deed

In respect of the Equity Mortgage advise each Purchaser on the terms of the Equity Mortgage and all their obligations and restrictions arising out of it (including but not limited to):

- The requirement to pay the management fee;

- When interest becomes payable and how this is calculated and increased;

- The redemption process and when the Repayment Sum is payable and how this is calculated;

- The restrictions on alterations, additions, change of use, subletting and any additional borrowing of any first charge mortgage.

Ensure that each Purchaser receives copies of these documents at least seven days before exchange of contracts.

Explain to each Purchaser their responsibilities, liabilities and obligations arising under the Equity Mortgage and in particular their obligations to pay the Repayment Sum and other sums to us. Advise each Purchaser of:

- The consequences of making a false statement;
- That the Property is at risk if they do not make the payments required by the Equity Mortgage; and
- The role of the Equity Loan Administrator and their role in administering the Equity Mortgage.

As you can see this is quite a lot that we need to provide the client with. However if you are organised it can be presented succinctly to a buyer and need not take up a huge amount of time. The key is being able to get this to a buy early as possible. In new build conveyancing, as a I hopefully established in the earlier chapters, speed is of the essence.

So you have done all of the above, what happens next? Well once you have a copy of your clients mortgage offer you can apply for the authority to exchange using the wonderfully names solicitors form 1 undertaking. Certain documents need to accompany solicitors form 1 and they are:

- The first-time buyer's declaration
- The buyer's identification documents
- A copy of the buyer's source of funds
- A copy of the UK Finance Disclosure of Incentives form – see my earlier comments over the same
- A copy of the mortgage offer and if available
- A copy of the valuation report

All of the above must accompany the form 1 certificate which is as I have stated is an undertaking.

Now before we go on to what happens once you have an ATE (Authority to Exchange) it is important to understand the complexities of the above process. I say this but here is the secret people, it is not that complicated. How difficult is it to get your clients to complete the paperwork listed? It is not that hard is it really? It is a few pieces of paper or in some cases some simple documents you should already have on file.

All conveyancers should have identification for their clients on file and of course evidence of their source of funds. It is usually one of the first things requested so not that hard to have and you must have it. Most buyers will have already had to provide that to the Estate Agents to show they have funds to buy the property or at least they have the deposit or in some cases to the developer. They will certainly had to provide evidence of their deposit in some format to their mortgage advisor, bank or financial advisor. The information is to hand so it is not arduous. Perhaps a touch monotonous at times but not the proverbial rocket science.

It is key to check that the mortgage offer matches what the property says it will be. If the address is slightly wrong then expect a problem with the Help to Buy Agent. The Agent has the thankless task of abiding by the rules set by Homes England so it is important that they do. If they do not meet the standards Homes England set then they risk being removed as the Agent thus costing jobs. Please keep this in mind rather than blaming them that you have not spotted that the mortgage offer is one pound (£1.00) out. Yes in reality it should not really matter but as set out above with their use of the English language the reality is the world of Homes England and that must be adhered to no matter what.

The UK Finance Mortgage Lenders Handbook Disclosure of Incentives form must also be correct. Top tip, make sure it is signed! The number I have seen over the years that are not signed which cause issues is huge. It takes a few seconds to check so please do. For my friends at the Help to Buy Agents I know that I can be guilty of missing the same so sorry in advance.

The classic issue though is that the equity deed has not been signed correctly. Now I know that is not a document that needs to be sent to obtain an Authority to Exchange but it is important that you get it signed bright and early to save issues later on. By saying it has not been signed correctly it is usually witnessed correctly. I appreciate we have had "lockdowns" of late but we all have neighbours we could see at a social distance to witness signatures.

Sad but my classic story from a client on the Isle of Wight always comes to mind. She called me and asked who could be her witness. I said "not a relative". She asked if her Mother would be a relative so I said yes. She asked if her Father would be a relative and said she should ask her Mother. I never did find out what the reply was.........

I should also mention that the legal advisors to the good people at Homes England have decided that the latest incarnation of Help to Buy should have some more quirks. Firstly that section 121 of the Law of Property Act 1925 in relation to rent charges should be banished from any transfer document that is going to have a Help to Buy charge. You will find a chapter later to explain what this rather obscure piece of legislation actually entails.

In addition it has been decreed that a local search should be carried out. As you will see in the chapter on searches I am rather an advocate of insurance but it seems that Homes England want to help out their friends at local authorities. All members of the same union perhaps? Regulated/personal searches can be used but only if absolutely you have to. I really do despair about a scheme that is designed to help first-time buyers get on the housing ladder. It is expensive enough but some people seem keen to make it even more expensive for them.

So moving on, you now have the golden ticket for your client which is the authority to exchange. Remember that the developer under the scheme can only ask for five percent (5%) at exchange less any reservation fee. The developer cannot take a bigger reservation fee or more deposit without the consent of Homes England first.

No matter how hard I seem to try and do find with certain clients that they cannot grasp that our idea from a conveyancing perspective of what a deposit is and their ideas are different. "I am putting down fifteen percent (15%) not five percent (5%)" is often the cry. I am not saying I have the magic answer to this but I have tried hard to refine the message over the years so I shall leave you to what works best for you.

So you have exchanged. Time to breathe a sigh of relief? No. Firstly you must inform the Help to Buy Agent that exchange has taken place. This is by way of a confirmation to exchange letter (CEF). Not complicated or too detailed but needs to be done.

It is worth confirming that an authority to proceed (ATP) is valid for three months, so your client has three months to exchange once it is issued. An authority to exchange is valid for the time stated on the same but normally around a month from when it was issued. Once exchange has taken place the property should be ready within six months for completion.

So after exchange you twiddle your thumbs and wait for the developer to confirm that the property is completed. No doubt during this time your client may contact you to say that the developer's sales representative has said that they should contact you to get a date for completion. Of course as you are working on site laying the bricks, connecting the pipes and sorting out the final ground works so are unable to answer that call at that time.

Once a completion date has been set, course ninety-nine times out of one hundred on the developer's terms various things have to be set into motion under the Help to Buy scheme. Namely that the fantastically named solicitors form 2 has to be completed and submitted to the Help to Buy agent.

This is another undertaking. What another I can sense the shouting now? Yes another one. Accept it or choose not to do this type of work. This is much easier, at least I think it is, than the solicitors form 1 undertaking.

Details of the transaction need to be regurgitated again onto a set format. The buyer's details mortgage details and date of completion need to be confirmed.

Unlike the previous version of Help to Buy the latest version requires a direct debit mandate to be provided by the solicitors to the Help to Buy Agent to collect the monthly administration fee of one pound (£1.00) and the future interest payments due after five years from the start date of the loan. I have to say looking back to the first Help to Buy loans I completed in 2013 I always wondered how they planned to get paid back their interest if the loan was not redeemed. Clearly Homes England have learned their lesson.

Once it is all completed then you have the obligatory unrealistic expectation of having everything registered promptly at HM Land Registry because we all know how ultra efficient they are at dealing with new build properties. As their technology has evolved to be even greater the time frame to process anything for a new title gets slower and slower. Ironic?

The Help to Buy agent must be provided with a copy of the dated equity deed (make sure you date all the pages correctly), a copy of your AP 1 form and evidence it has been submitted to HM Land Registry ideally as well. Hopefully by 2076 the application will have been returned.

So is this a hard process? No it is not but some lawyers seem to make heavy going of it. It is a process. Follow the process and you will be fine. If you stick to driving on the left there are no accidents, that is how my mind works on these things.

I do though have this to say about the new scheme. The price differences between regions are unfair. Under the old scheme provided the price was below six hundred thousand pounds it was not an issue. That applied if you were in Newcastle upon Tyne or Newcastle under Lyme. The 2021-2023 scheme changes all of that.

The Country is split into regions with the following arrangements price wise:

Region	Full Purchase Price Cap
East of England	£407,400
East Midlands	£261,900
London	£600,000
North East	£186,100
North West	£224,400
South East	£437,600
South West	£349,000
West Midlands	£255,600
Yorkshire and The Humber	£228,100.00

Now this may seem fair to some but I think it does create inequality as I live in Hampshire which is considered South East but one mile up the road from my house would take me into Wiltshire. That is nearly a one hundred thousand price difference for the upper limit of Help to Buy between the two bordering counties.

I do worry that the Help to Buy scheme as it has now been created will benefit the much bigger developers rather than all who had access to it before. Not really a legal point but one worth making.

Now at the time of writing the Help to buy scheme has been extended in relation to the rules as to when the property has to be build complete. In 2022 it was announced that properties had to be build complete as in signed off by building control for occupation by December 2022. That was extended to January 2023 and has now been extended until 17 March 2023. It may well be extended for a further time period to allow completions to take place. There continue to be large delays with infrastructure assembly (connections to utilities etc) and supply chain issues with the supply for electrical components as well as a plethora of other items crucial to a modern home.

In summary, Help to Buy is a great scheme. That is not just my opinion. It has helped thousands on to the housing market and created billions of pounds for our economy which helps everyone in the long term. Yes some changes were needed which have been made. I agree it should be limited to first time buyers.

The concern is that there is no immediate scheme to replace it. One of the few things that our beloved politicians agree upon is we need more property. How to deliver it and who should control it is up for debate but there is a broad agreement more homes are needed. If the Help to Buy scheme has added £10,000.00 per property that has been sold under the project into the wider economy then are we not missing a trick in replacing the scheme now? I am a gambling man and expect we may well see a similar scheme within the next few years as it worked so well. The developers are likely to be lobbying for the same. Say it quietly, but I will be joining them in pushing for something else as I personally think it is needed.

What conveyancers need to realise is that it is not hard. Just go with the flow and it will be fine. Moving on from Help to Buy we will now look at the pitfalls of the dreaded Estate Rent Charges. They're really not that bad when you know what to look out for.

CHAPTER EIGHT

ESTATE CHARGES

Paul Sams

Given that Local authorities do not have much by way of funding as they like to tell us, some more than others, roads on new estates are rarely adopted. Roads are expensive to maintain and Councils would dearly like to not have to pay out for the same. Potholes are expensive to fill in and are awkward to get to.

Therefore anything built as a new build property in the past twenty years or so is likely to have an estate charge upon it. This is a yearly rent charge which allows the developer to ensure that the estate residents all generally are part of a management company handed over to them so they can enjoy the shared responsibility happily together. Obviously this does not happen as people moan like mad about the charges they face which then ends up in certain mainstream media being disproportionally represented.

That is not what I want to look at in this chapter in any real detail. I would add that it is worth pointing out to your client that if it is an owner lead management company that most will be they all have a say in how it is run so can vote or even better volunteer to be a Director to ensure they have their say. If they do not do that then more fool them.

What I do want to do is to have a look at rent charges and particular the issues they can cause because of a slightly obscure part of the Law of Property Act 1925. My Partner Emma Menzies always chuckles when I use this phrase but on older estates where the rent charge has been established for some time this is very much "spilt milk under the bridge". On new estates you are dealing with now though you can do something about it to make sure that your clients title is suitable for their mortgage lender(s).

Now on one of those rare occasions I need to quote the law. If this was a webinar it is probably the time you would go to make a cup of tea or take a comfort break. Prepare yourselves, here goes.

The Rentcharges Act 1977 provides that, since 22 August 1977, only the following types of rentcharges can be created:

- estate rentcharges (s2(3)(c));
- a rentcharge for the life of a person or a shorter period charged on land which is held in trust for giving effect to the charge under the Trusts of Land and Appointment of Trustees Act 1996 (s2(3)(a) of RcA 1977);
- a rentcharge under any statute providing for the creation of rentcharges in connection with the execution of works on land (s2(3)(d)); and
- a rentcharge created by, or in accordance with the requirement of, a court order (s2(3)(e)).
- a rentcharge which would have had that effect but for the fact that the land on which the rent is charged is settled land or subject to a trust of land (s2(3)(b));

All rentcharges are considered as accruing from day to day and can be apportioned in respect of time unless expressly stated otherwise (s7 Apportinment Act 1870). I am sure that is an act that you are all intimately familiar with.

Until 6 April 2014 it was the case that an unregistered rentcharge was wholly extinguished following the expiration of 12 years from the date on which the right of action to recover it accrued to the rent owner.

Following the amendments made by the Tribunals, Courts and Enforcement Act 2007, rentcharges are now treated as 'rent' for the purposes of the Limitation Act 1980.

So why should you care about these gloriously modern Acts of Parliament? Well it is because ninety times out of one hundred the new build property you will be acting on the purchase for will have a rent charge. As you all know positive covenants do not run with the land. A rent charge does so this gets around that issue very cleverly. What is not to like with such a scheme. It achieves what it wants and resolves any issues?

Sadly there is an issue that comes from this and it is this. It is section 121 of the Law of Property Act 1925. This came to mass attention, not quite front page of the Sunday Times (other news publications are available) but certainly to the Legal world's attention with the case of Roberts v Lawton [2016] UKUT 395.

This case involved a company whose business is to buy and manage rentcharges. The company owned about 15,000 rentcharges. The company used its statutory enforcement rights under section 121 LPA 1925, to compel property owners to make payment of arrears and significant costs.

So what are the statutory powers you all shout together in an alto tone? Well the following remedies may be available to a rent owner where arrears have accrued:-

- a right of re-entry;
- entry onto the land to take the income from it or to hold the land until arrears have been discharged;
- grant of a lease of the land charged on trust to raise arrears;
- a claim on the covenant;

- a claim for a debt;
- sale or mortgage of the land charged;
- appointment of a receiver; or
- service of a statutory demand

The Lawton case involved a number of property owners who were in arrears with their rentcharges for various small amounts; the lowest was six pounds (£6.00) and the highest fifteen pounds (£15.00). The company granted its directors, as trustees, rentcharge leases of for a term of 99 years that reserved no rent and applied to register the leases at the Land Registry. This is handily provided for in section 121 (4) of the Law of Property Act 1925.

Once registered, these leases would, stymie the sale of these properties because sale would not be practically viable, even if the tenant directors did not seek to take possession. The landowners were compelled to pay significant sums in return for surrender of the leases. One owner had been asked to pay six hundred and fifty pounds (£650.00). This is on a rent charge of six pounds per annum. That is a mark up of one hundred times it's yearly value. Even where the rent charge is paid, the lease continues.

The Land Registry initially refused to register the leases and the case came before the Upper Tribunal to decide whether the rentcharge leases were registrable. The Tribunal Judge reluctantly found that the practise was lawful despite being a disproportionate and unfair remedy.

Judge Elizabeth Cook said: "Once the lease is in existence, therefore, it amounts to a stranglehold on the property owner whose freehold is worthless in the presence of the lease."

Now there are two ways to look at this. The way most take it is this horrendous and should be stopped. It is prejudicing hard working folk who have worked hard to purchase their home. I agree although I do have a wry smile come across my face when I think of the other way. How smart were the company who purchased all these rent charges to take advantage of the same. You have to stop and applaud them in a way for legally working this out. Clearly their legal representation was very sharp.

So section 121 of the Law of Property Act 1925 is an issue. Owners do not want a lease against their freehold title and neither do lenders. If you need more evidence of what lenders views on the matter is then read section 5.15 of the UK Finance Mortgage Lenders Handbook on the topic.

Now I appreciate that every lender treats it differently but the best way to deal with it is to remove the threat of the same. Developers are not fools and they have to sell to make money. Therefore they have all started to modify their titles to ensure that this threat is negated. This has been expedited by the fact that under the new Help to Buy scheme which will run until at least 2023 that it is an absolute requirements that parts three and four of section 121 of the Law of Property Act 1925 are specifically excluded.

The difficulty of course comes from the times that you may be unsure it is a rent charge or not. I appreciate that sometimes this may not be easy to tell but as I like to say on my courses, if it looks like a duck and quacks like a duck it is probably a duck. However keep in mind that not all ducks quack like the Muscovy duck. In fact although the Muscovy duck looks like a duck not only does it not quack but the genetics of the same suggest it is more a kind of water fowl that is completely different to other ducks. Anyway enough about ducks but you get my point I hope.

A quick alternative to a deed of variation to a rent charge is of course our old friend, legal indemnity insurance. For a relatively cheap price and quick result indemnity insurance can be obtained for a competitive price. The issue of course is that some lenders will not accept the same. The bigger issue though is that insurance covers if something goes wrong. Surely it is better to modify the same and remove the threat to protect your client and any future lender client?

Modern transfers will be modified, or at least should be to remove this as an issue. Estate charges are not the evil they are portrayed to be though. They serve a purpose and if they are respected you can confidently allow your client to purchase.

I strongly suspect that at some point in the near future some super sharp civil servant will suggest that we have a new Law of Property Act. The one we have from 1925 with it's various modifications probably now needs a whole new act to replace it rather than running repairs. A simple solution to the issues caused under section 121 and it's potentially draconian remedies would be to amend the legislation itself. Perhaps I am being too optimistic in wishing for this.

Well enough of this frivolity let us move to the next and most important chapter – completion. I say this is the most important bit as it is when clients can move into their dream home and we as lawyers get paid!

CHAPTER NINE

COMPLETION

Rebecca East

It's all good and well saying exchange of contracts is the aim (well it is for developers anyway) but realistically completion is the most important part as this is the point where clients can move into their dream home and we get our legal fees paid. Sounds simple doesn't it? There is in fact a lot of work that goes on behind the scenes to prepare a file for completion. This is something I think a lot of people (clients mainly!) forget. Maybe it's a good thing that it seems a well-oiled machine on the day? Who knows!

Depending on whether you agreed to complete on notice or whether you were given a fixed completion date the steps between the point in which you exchange to completion are fairly similar but do have certain differences.

The majority of new build homes are still being built at the point in which you exchange contracts. This means that completion will often be on notice with the developer. But what does this mean for completion? Exchange of contracts will take place and instead of inserting a fixed completion date into the contract it will specify the anticipated build date and the termination period (or longstop date as it is also known). Within the contract there will be notice provisions which will give you a set number of days the developer's solicitor must give you when serving you with notice. This can be 10 working days or earlier by agreement.

Whilst the ALCD and longstop dates give you a rough indication of when completion is likely to happen it does not give you a specific date which means you will be waiting for notice to be served by the developer's solicitor before you can submit mortgage funds, submit Form 2 and prepare financial statements. In these such instances, I advise my clients on exchange to keep in regular contact with the site offices for the developer as they will be able to give regular updates to my client regarding the build stage and likely completion date.

Once a property has been signed off and is ready for occupation the developer's solicitor will serve you notice to complete with set completion date. As I said above, it is likely that your client will be chomping at the bit to complete ASAP so be prepared to drop everything (quite literally sometimes) in order that your file is prepared in good time for completion. In a situation where an earlier date has been agreed for completion, always be conscious about the likelihood of getting mortgage funds, a priority search result and, where applicable, your TD from Help to Buy in time for completion.

Now as discussed in chapter 7, you will need to keep an eye on your client's mortgage offer expiration date. It is useful to put this in your calendar and as the expiration date nears but no sign of the property being ready for occupation, you will need to ensure your client is in talks with the broker regarding extension. On some occasion recently the mortgage broker has actually contacted me to say that the lender will extend but they will require a letter from us (emailed or faxed… don't use snail mail) confirming we have exchanged and how long the extension we require is for. The likes of Nationwide usually extend for a further 6 weeks on new build properties (sometimes longer) but they will need request for extension no later than 2 weeks prior to the expiration date.

It is not only the mortgage expiration date you need to be wary of, a change in financial market or change in client's personal or financial circumstances may mean a new mortgage offer or extension is not able to be offered. As mentioned in chapter 7, you need to be raising this risk with your clients from the outset really so they are aware long before the property is built and they suddenly realise they can't secure mortgage finance.

Once notice has been served I instantly have a metaphorical tick list ready in my head of the next steps. First step always is tell your clients notice has been served and what the completion date is. I tend to do this verbally and in writing (by email.) Sounds blatantly obvious to suggest that but you can get so involved with all the steps required to get this matter to completion that is a simple mistake to make. I always follow up this by phone and email so they can deny that they are aware. Next I submit mortgage funds, submit Form 2 (if applicable) to Help to Buy and submit my bankruptcy and priority searches.

Second step is to check I have all the necessary signed paperwork from my client. Whilst I try and get the client to sign all paperwork before exchange, it is always good to check you have all paperwork signed including Transfer Deed, Help to Buy Equity Deed (if applicable) and mortgage deed. If not, get these sent as soon as possible and advise the clients they need to sign and return hard copies before completion. I'm sure all conveyancing practitioners at some point have realised late on that they don't have the necessary signed mortgage deed or that there isn't a witness signature on the Transfer. Next I then look at the financial aspect of the transaction in terms of whether I need money from my client or if there will be money due from them.

Unlike second-hand market properties, the requirement for buildings insurance falls to the buyer on completion and not exchange of contracts. You will need to mention to your client once notice is served that they should be shopping around for suitable products so they can put this on risk from the day of completion. This is obviously quite important but can be missed in the excitement of moving day.

A further distinct difference between second-hand market properties and that of new build is that you will need a completion statement from the developer's solicitor before you can finalise your financial statement to your client. This does tend to follow once notice is served but if not you might want to give it a quick chase.

What I will say about developer's completion statements are that they're not always right. Now we are all human and we make mistakes, but it is worth checking the maths first to make sure you don't come into any difficulties late in the day. If this sounds like I am talking from experience I most certainly am. Yes, their statement was wrong, but I didn't check it so that made me similarly responsible, but it also meant my statement to my client was wrong so watch out. It is also worth cross checking the Help to Buy advance especially if the purchase price has changed during the course of the transaction as this will affect the advance amount.

Once that has been checked and you've sent your statement to your client, wait and see how long it will be before you get asked *"what's an engrossment fee?" "Why am I paying service charges upfront when the development isn't finalised yet?"* Ah, now if I had a pound for every time I was asked these two questions, I would also be a millionaire! As Paul said above in chapter 2, you can colour it, highlight it, put it in bold etc but the clients will not see these points in the report (even if you've asked them to sign a copy of the report to confirm they have read the same!)

With second-hand market properties you'll find that you will receive or request to have replies to standard requisitions on title (form TA13). With new build transactions this tends to be contained in the preliminary information form from the outset. You'll want to check the position with any charges on the title to ensure you are provided with the relevant discharges after completion and also carry out lawyer checker on the bank details (as these are usually provided by email). It remains good practice to do this anyway.

If I just have a purchase transaction without related sale and I have all the necessary completion funds in the day before completion, I ask the developer's solicitor if I can send funds a day early. Why I hear you ask? Well, most clients want to get the keys ASAP on the day of completion, and this means it is one thing less for you to do on the day and the client generally can get the keys to the property very early on the day of completion.

So we've now got clients completion funds and mortgage advance and we have sent the amount shown on the developer's statement to their client account. What next? You contact the developer's solicitor to ask them for confirmation of receipt of funds and ask if keys can now be released to our client. My absolute favourite part of conveyancing without fail is the day you can call your client and tell them they've completed and they can collect keys. Most of the time an Estate Agent or Site office has beaten you to it but nonetheless it still is my favourite part. If you're lucky you'll get a squeal of excitement (which does always make my day!) but most of the time it is just that simple "thank you" from the client that reminds you why you put yourself through the stress and strain that is conveyancing.

The final completion stage is to send your clients signed Transfer Deed and signed plans to the developer's solicitor. I say final as the rest of the steps that follow I'd consider to fall under the post-completion process of which I won't go into for the purposes of this chapter. The developer's solicitor is unlikely to release their signed Transfer to you to enable registration at HM Land Registry until they have received your clients signed part so with your standard completion letter to the developer's solicitor, get this sent as well.

Well that's it. You've reached completion. You can breathe a sigh of relief (we won't talk about the Land Registry registration requirement however ha!) Can you believe all of that can happen in such a short space of time (especially if the property is built). The fastest I've ever dealt with a new build purchase with no chain was 5 working days from receipt of reservation form to completion. Realistically I could have completed this sooner but the clients wanted to complete on the Thursday as opposed to the Tuesday. Would have been 3 working days otherwise. Provided you have a client who is willing to return paperwork ASAP, a developer who is there to work with you and your client with getting the necessary information to their conveyancing practitioner in a timely manner then anything is possible. Teamwork is key with conveyancing. Whilst it can sometimes feel like you're working against one another, you're not. We're all working to the same objective and as I've said above, clients just want to be able to move into their new home. Everything else is unnecessary in their eyes. Houses are more than bricks and mortar, they symbolise a new start for couples and families. It is only then that you start to understand why there is so much emotion and stress involved for clients.

CHAPTER TEN

CONCLUSION

Rebecca East & Paul Sams

Well if you've got to this point that is a good sign as it means you haven't fallen asleep or simply stopped reading. I appreciate this may be a dry subject to some but we hope this guide gives you, the reader, practical information to enable you to conduct a new build conveyancing matter with confidence. This book aims to serve you with a vital insight into the process involved with new build conveyancing and what to look out for during the course of the transaction to ensure there are no unnecessary delays. Whilst the processes involved with new build and second-hand market transactions are pretty much similar (sorry to break it to you so many pages later!) there are distinct differences which we hope you are now aware of.

So the next time your client asks what a conveyancing practitioner does and what purpose they have, slide them a copy of this book (or suggest that they buy a copy instead!) Hopefully they will realise quite how much work and knowledge goes into buying a house.

Thank you for taking the time out of your day to read this book. I'll hand you over to Paul now to have the final word.

Well has this not been fun? Not quite a page turning thriller on religious imagery or a tale of debauchery for the millennials but hopefully you have found it interesting. The biggest thing I would say as the difference between the new build conveyancing and resale properties can be summed up in the words of a legend who said "it is all about speed". When that wise person was Sonic the Hedgehog then you may doubt my sincerity.

I am though very serious. A major developer has targets to hit all the way through the process of acquiring, sourcing, building then selling a new home. They don't have time (pardon the pun) to waste and could punish your client if you do not get the property exchanged in time. Yes quite often they will make what you consider ludicrous requests in relation to the timing of matters. However at the end of the day they are property professionals. If you are acting for a client and there is a deadline which you know you will not hit for some reason then let me give you one final tip.

Do you know what that is? Pick the phone up and speak to their solicitors or better yet speak to the developer direct to explain what the issue is. As they are professionals they will listen. If you give them a solid reason why their deadline will not be met and what you will do to resolve it plus a time frame to resolve it in I am fairly certain they will agree to extend the deadline. You just need to ask and have a reason. You may be surprised how accommodating they will be if they know the facts of things.

I do hope you have found this useful. Failing that, if you do not want to deal with new build property just let us know, we love them!

MORE BOOKS BY LAW BRIEF PUBLISHING

A selection of our other titles available now:-

'A Practical Guide to Parental Alienation in Private and Public Law Children Cases' by Sam King QC & Frankie Shama
'Contested Heritage – Removing Art from Land and Historic Buildings' by Richard Harwood QC, Catherine Dobson, David Sawtell
'The Limits of Separate Legal Personality: When Those Running a Company Can Be Held Personally Liable for Losses Caused to Third Parties Outside of the Company' by Dr Mike Wilkinson
'A Practical Guide to Transgender Law' by Robin Moira White & Nicola Newbegin
'Artificial Intelligence – The Practical Legal Issues (2nd Edition)' by John Buyers
'A Practical Guide to Residential Freehold Conveyancing' by Lorraine Richardson
'A Practical Guide to Pensions on Divorce for Lawyers' by Bryan Scant
'A Practical Guide to Challenging Sham Marriage Allegations in Immigration Law' by Priya Solanki
'A Practical Guide to Legal Rights in Scotland' by Sarah-Jane Macdonald
'A Practical Guide to New Build Conveyancing' by Paul Sams & Rebecca East
'A Practical Guide to Defending Barristers in Disciplinary Cases' by Marc Beaumont
'A Practical Guide to Inherited Wealth on Divorce' by Hayley Trim
'A Practical Guide to Practice Direction 12J and Domestic Abuse in Private Law Children Proceedings' by Rebecca Cross & Malvika Jaganmohan
'A Practical Guide to Confiscation and Restraint' by Narita Bahra QC, John Carl Townsend, David Winch
'A Practical Guide to the Law of Forests in Scotland' by Philip Buchan
'A Practical Guide to Health and Medical Cases in Immigration Law' by Rebecca Chapman & Miranda Butler
'A Practical Guide to Bad Character Evidence for Criminal Practitioners by Aparna Rao
'A Practical Guide to Extradition Law post-Brexit' by Myles Grandison et al

'A Practical Guide to Hoarding and Mental Health for Housing Lawyers' by Rachel Coyle
'A Practical Guide to Psychiatric Claims in Personal Injury – 2nd Edition' by Liam Ryan
'Stephens on Contractual Indemnities' by Richard Stephens
'A Practical Guide to the EU Succession Regulation' by Richard Frimston
'A Practical Guide to Solicitor and Client Costs – 2nd Edition' by Robin Dunne
'Constructive Dismissal – Practice Pointers and Principles' by Benjimin Burgher
'A Practical Guide to Religion and Belief Discrimination Claims in the Workplace' by Kashif Ali
'A Practical Guide to the Law of Medical Treatment Decisions' by Ben Troke
'Fundamental Dishonesty and QOCS in Personal Injury Proceedings: Law and Practice' by Jake Rowley
'A Practical Guide to the Law in Relation to School Exclusions' by Charlotte Hadfield & Alice de Coverley
'A Practical Guide to Divorce for the Silver Separators' by Karin Walker
'The Right to be Forgotten – The Law and Practical Issues' by Melissa Stock
'A Practical Guide to Planning Law and Rights of Way in National Parks, the Broads and AONBs' by James Maurici QC, James Neill et al
'A Practical Guide to Election Law' by Tom Tabori
'A Practical Guide to the Law in Relation to Surrogacy' by Andrew Powell
'A Practical Guide to Claims Arising from Fatal Accidents – 2nd Edition' by James Patience
'A Practical Guide to the Ownership of Employee Inventions – From Entitlement to Compensation' by James Tumbridge & Ashley Roughton
'A Practical Guide to Asbestos Claims' by Jonathan Owen & Gareth McAloon
'A Practical Guide to Stamp Duty Land Tax in England and Northern Ireland' by Suzanne O'Hara
'A Practical Guide to the Law of Farming Partnerships' by Philip Whitcomb
'Covid-19, Homeworking and the Law – The Essential Guide to Employment and GDPR Issues' by Forbes Solicitors
'Covid-19 and Criminal Law – The Essential Guide' by Ramya Nagesh
'Covid-19 and Family Law in England and Wales – The Essential Guide' by Safda Mahmood

'A Practical Guide to the Law of Unlawful Eviction and Harassment – 2nd Edition' by Stephanie Lovegrove

'Covid-19, Brexit and the Law of Commercial Leases – The Essential Guide' by Mark Shelton

'A Practical Guide to Costs in Personal Injury Claims – 2nd Edition' by Matthew Hoe

'A Practical Guide to the General Data Protection Regulation (GDPR) – 2nd Edition' by Keith Markham

'Ellis on Credit Hire – Sixth Edition' by Aidan Ellis & Tim Kevan

'A Practical Guide to Working with Litigants in Person and McKenzie Friends in Family Cases' by Stuart Barlow

'Protecting Unregistered Brands: A Practical Guide to the Law of Passing Off' by Lorna Brazell

'A Practical Guide to Secondary Liability and Joint Enterprise Post-Jogee' by Joanne Cecil & James Mehigan

'A Practical Guide to the Pre-Action RTA Claims Protocol for Personal Injury Lawyers' by Antonia Ford

'A Practical Guide to Neighbour Disputes and the Law' by Alexander Walsh

'A Practical Guide to Forfeiture of Leases' by Mark Shelton

'A Practical Guide to Coercive Control for Legal Practitioners and Victims' by Rachel Horman

'A Practical Guide to Rights Over Airspace and Subsoil' by Daniel Gatty

'Tackling Disclosure in the Criminal Courts – A Practitioner's Guide' by Narita Bahra QC & Don Ramble

'A Practical Guide to the Law of Driverless Cars – Second Edition' by Alex Glassbrook, Emma Northey & Scarlett Milligan

'A Practical Guide to TOLATA Claims' by Greg Williams

'A Practical Guide to Elderly Law – 2nd Edition' by Justin Patten

'A Practical Guide to Responding to Housing Disrepair and Unfitness Claims' by Iain Wightwick

'A Practical Guide to the Construction and Rectification of Wills and Trust Instruments' by Edward Hewitt

'A Practical Guide to the Law of Bullying and Harassment in the Workplace' by Philip Hyland

'How to Be a Freelance Solicitor: A Practical Guide to the SRA-Regulated Freelance Solicitor Model' by Paul Bennett

'A Practical Guide to Prison Injury Claims' by Malcolm Johnson
'A Practical Guide to the Small Claims Track - 2nd Edition' by Dominic Bright
'A Practical Guide to Advising Clients at the Police Station' by Colin Stephen McKeown-Beaumont
'A Practical Guide to Antisocial Behaviour Injunctions' by Iain Wightwick
'Practical Mediation: A Guide for Mediators, Advocates, Advisers, Lawyers, and Students in Civil, Commercial, Business, Property, Workplace, and Employment Cases' by Jonathan Dingle with John Sephton
'The Mini-Pupillage Workbook' by David Boyle
'A Practical Guide to Crofting Law' by Brian Inkster
'A Practical Guide to Spousal Maintenance' by Liz Cowell
'A Practical Guide to the Law of Domain Names and Cybersquatting' by Andrew Clemson
'A Practical Guide to the Law of Gender Pay Gap Reporting' by Harini Iyengar
'A Practical Guide to the Rights of Grandparents in Children Proceedings' by Stuart Barlow
'NHS Whistleblowing and the Law' by Joseph England
'Employment Law and the Gig Economy' by Nigel Mackay & Annie Powell
'A Practical Guide to Noise Induced Hearing Loss (NIHL) Claims' by Andrew Mckie, Ian Skeate, Gareth McAloon
'An Introduction to Beauty Negligence Claims – A Practical Guide for the Personal Injury Practitioner' by Greg Almond
'Intercompany Agreements for Transfer Pricing Compliance' by Paul Sutton
'Zen and the Art of Mediation' by Martin Plowman
'A Practical Guide to the SRA Principles, Individual and Law Firm Codes of Conduct 2019 – What Every Law Firm Needs to Know' by Paul Bennett
'A Practical Guide to Adoption for Family Lawyers' by Graham Pegg
'A Practical Guide to Industrial Disease Claims' by Andrew Mckie & Ian Skeate
'A Practical Guide to Redundancy' by Philip Hyland
'A Practical Guide to Vicarious Liability' by Mariel Irvine
'A Practical Guide to Applications for Landlord's Consent and Variation of Leases' by Mark Shelton
'A Practical Guide to Relief from Sanctions Post-Mitchell and Denton' by Peter Causton

'A Practical Guide to Equity Release for Advisors' by Paul Sams
'A Practical Guide to Financial Services Claims' by Chris Hegarty
'The Law of Houses in Multiple Occupation: A Practical Guide to HMO Proceedings' by Julian Hunt
'Occupiers, Highways and Defective Premises Claims: A Practical Guide Post-Jackson – 2nd Edition' by Andrew Mckie
'A Practical Guide to Financial Ombudsman Service Claims' by Adam Temple & Robert Scrivenor
'A Practical Guide to Advising Schools on Employment Law' by Jonathan Holden
'A Practical Guide to Running Housing Disrepair and Cavity Wall Claims: 2nd Edition' by Andrew Mckie & Ian Skeate
'A Practical Guide to Holiday Sickness Claims – 2nd Edition' by Andrew Mckie & Ian Skeate
'Arguments and Tactics for Personal Injury and Clinical Negligence Claims' by Dorian Williams
'A Practical Guide to Drone Law' by Rufus Ballaster, Andrew Firman, Eleanor Clot
'A Practical Guide to Compliance for Personal Injury Firms Working With Claims Management Companies' by Paul Bennett
'RTA Allegations of Fraud in a Post-Jackson Era: The Handbook – 2nd Edition' by Andrew Mckie
'RTA Personal Injury Claims: A Practical Guide Post-Jackson' by Andrew Mckie
'On Experts: CPR35 for Lawyers and Experts' by David Boyle
'An Introduction to Personal Injury Law' by David Boyle

These books and more are available to order online direct from the publisher at www.lawbriefpublishing.com, where you can also read free sample chapters. For any queries, contact us on 0844 587 2383 or mail@lawbriefpublishing.com.

Our books are also usually in stock at www.amazon.co.uk with free next day delivery for Prime members, and at good legal bookshops such as Wildy & Sons.

We are regularly launching new books in our series of practical day-to-day practitioners' guides. Visit our website and join our free newsletter to be kept informed and to receive special offers, free chapters, etc.

You can also follow us on Twitter at www.twitter.com/lawbriefpub.

www.ingramcontent.com/pod-product-compliance
Lightning Source LLC
LaVergne TN
LVHW022110200926
848481LV00003B/1141
* 9 7 8 1 9 1 4 6 0 8 9 0 2 *